Artificial Paradises

Charles Baudelaire

Artificial Paradises

Translation, Introduction, and Notes by
Stacy Diamond

A Citadel Press Book
Published by Carol Publishing Group

A Citadel Press Book
Published by Carol Publishing Group
Citadel Press is a registered trademark of Carol Communications, Inc.

Editorial Offices: 600 Madison Avenue, New York, N.Y. 10022
Sales and Distribution Offices: 120 Enterprise Avenue, Secaucus, N.J. 07094
In Canada: Canadian Manda Group, One Atlantic Avenue, Suite 105, Toronto, Ontario M6K 3E7
Queries regarding rights and permissions should be addressed to Carol Publishing Group, 600 Madison Avenue, New York, N.Y. 10022

Carol Publishing Group books are available at special discounts for bulk purchases, sales promotion, fund-raising, or educational purposes. Special editions can be created to specifications. For details, contact: Special Sales Department, Carol Publishing Group, 120 Enterprise Avenue, Secaucus, N.J. 07094.

Manufactured in the United States of America
10 9 8 7 6 5 4 3 2 1

Library of Congress Cataloging-in-Publication Data

Baudelaire, Charles, 1821–1867.
    [Paradis artificiels. English]
    Artificial paradises: Baudelaire's masterpiece on hashish/
by Charles Baudelaire
        p.   cm.
    ISBN 0–8065–1483–3
    1. Hallucinogenic drugs. 2. Authors—Drug use. 3. Narcotic habit. 4. Hashish. I. Title
PQ2191.P3E58   1996
848'.807—dc20   94–17664
                                                         CIP

Contents

Introduction

BAUDELAIRE'S FIRST VOLUME of verse, *Les Fleurs du mal*, was published in Paris in June of 1857. The French critics of the day, led most truculently by *Le Figaro*, joined together to asperse the poet's moral character. The noise raised by that loud community led to his trial and conviction (20 August) for offenses against public morality. Damned and condemned, with six of his verses banned,[1] Baudelaire paid the odious slanderers little heed. That his work roused such hostility was in part a good sign. To his mother he wrote:

> You know that I have never viewed literature and the arts in any other light than as pursuing an end foreign to morality, and that the beauties of conception and style are enough for me. But this book, entitled *Les Fleurs du mal*, as you shall see, is clothed in a cold and sinister beauty; it was written with fury and patience. Indeed the proof of its unmistakable value lies in the scorn being heaped upon it. The book enrages people.[2]

Gustave Flaubert, the brilliant author of *Madame Bovary*, had been tried on obscenity charges earlier the same year. Upon receiving a copy of *Les Paradis artificiels*, he expressed his admiration in these terms:

> You are very kind, my dear Baudelaire, to have sent me such

---

1. The French tribunal banned the following six poems: "Les Bijoux," "Le Léthé," "A Celle qui est trop gaie," "Lesbos," "Les Femmes damnées," and "Les Metamorphoses du vampire." The poet was also fined three hundred francs. For a full account of the incident, see Enid Starkie's *Baudelaire* (London, 1957).

2. Letter, 9 July 1857.

a book! I am pleased with the whole of it, intention, style, even the paper. I read it most attentively. But I must especially thank you for introducing me to Mr. De Quincey, a charming man! How likable he is!

Here (to dispense with the *buts*) is my sole objection. It appears to me that by treating such a subject so distantly, in a work that is the beginning of a science, in a work of observation and induction, you have (and many times over) insisted too much(?) on *the Spirit of Evil.* One can sense a leavening of Catholicism here and there. I would have preferred that you *not blame* hashish, opium, and excess. Do you know what will come of them later?

But understand that this is a *personal* opinion and thus of small account. I do not in the least recognize the right of the critic to substitute his thoughts for those of another. — And is not that which I criticize in your book perhaps that which constitutes its originality, and the very mark of your talent? Do not resemble your fellow man—that is everything. Now that I have given vent to my malice, I know not how to express the full extent of my admiration for your work, which I found excellent from beginning to end. The style is forceful, firm, and very searching...

As for the section entitled "An Opium-Eater," I do not know how deeply you are indebted to De Quincey—but in any case, what a marvel! No one could be nicer, at least so it seems.

For some time these drugs have, for me, exerted a certain attraction. I even possess some excellent hashish, prepared for me by the pharmacist Gastinel. But *it frightens me*—and for this I blame myself.

Are you familiar with Escayrac de Lauture's *Soudan?*[3]

---

3. Comte d'Escayrac de Lauture, *Le Désert et le Soudan,* Paris, 1853.

Here one finds a whole private theogony and cosmogony fashioned by an opium-smoker. I, for my part, remember it with some amusement, but I prefer Mr. De Quincey. The poor man! and whatever became of Miss Ann! You should be complimented as well for your little note relative to moral critics. There, I have already been scratched or rather stroked in my sensitive spot. I impatiently await your *New flowers of Evil.**

How hard you work! And how well!

Goodbye. I shake your hand and slap your shoulder.
G[ustave] Flaubert

*My observation might be inappropriate here. For the poet is perfectly within his rights to believe whatsoever he wishes. But the philosophic man?

Is this unwisely spoken? I am clear about it myself, nevertheless. We shall discuss it soon.[4]

Baudelaire, reflecting on the nature of the Spirit of Evil, which he saw as arising from a cause altogether outside of the individual, replied to Flaubert the following day:

My dear Flaubert, I thank you most gratefully for your excellent letter. I was struck by your observation and, having descended very sincerely into the recollection of my musings, I realize that I had been continually obsessed by an inability to accept certain of man's deeds or actions without the hypothesis that malevolent powers, external to himself, of themselves intervene. Even were the entire nineteenth century in league against me, I would not retract this significant admission. I reserve the right to change my mind, however, or to contradict myself at any time.

Feeling an affinity with Swedenborgian theory, Baudelaire

---

4. Letter, 25 June 1860.

describes, in his sonnet "Correspondances," the links by which the external world is bound to the world of the spirit:

Le Nature est un temple où de vivants piliers
Laissent parfois sortir de confuses paroles;
L'homme y passe à travers des forêts de symboles
Qui l'observent avec des regards familiers.

Comme de longs échos qui de loin se confondent
Dans une ténébreuse et profonde unité,
Vaste comme la nuit et comme la clarté,
Les parfums, les couleurs et les sons se répondent.

Paul Verlaine, a genius in the art of poetic instrumentation, elaborates on this theory: "Why should not the Poet translate colors and sounds, once he has determined the colors of the vowels, and why should not his magic then reach as far as the consonants, all combining to form an intelligent, multicolored Orchestra?"

Having little faith in inspiration, Baudelaire recommends hard work: "I believe only in patient work, the truth spoken in good French and the magic of the correct word." The writer must always be precise, must always find the perfect form of expression, or else renounce the pen: "If the word doesn't exist, invent it; but first be sure that it doesn't exist." Poetry, for Baudelaire, was never the spontaneous overflow of feeling. Beauty, he believed, is always the product of artistic effort; nature must be elevated beyond impassioned expression: "The bad is produced effortlessly, as something which is inevitable; the good is always the result of an art."

Baudelaire formulated his poetic theory nowhere more clearly than in the preface to his beautiful translation of Edgar Allan Poe (*Nouvelles Notes sur Edgar Poe,* 1857). Here Baudelaire restates segments of Poe's *Poetic Principle:*

That pleasure which is at once the most pure, the most

elevating, and the most intense, is derived, I maintain, from the contemplation of the Beautiful. In the contemplation of Beauty we alone find it possible to attain that pleasurable elevation, or excitement, of the soul, which we recognize as the Poetic Sentiment, and which is so easily distinguished from Truth, which is the satisfaction of the Reason, or from Passion, which is the excitement of the heart. I make Beauty, therefore—using the word as inclusive of the sublime—I make Beauty the province of the poem, simply because it is an obvious rule of Art that effects should be made to spring as directly as possible from their causes:—no one as yet having been weak enough to deny that the peculiar elevation in question is at least most readily attainable in the poem. It by no means follows, however, that the incitements of Passion, or the precepts of Duty, or even the lessons of Truth, may not be introduced into a poem, and with advantage; for they may subserve, incidentally, in various ways, the general purposes of the work:—but the true artist will always contrive to tone them down in proper subjection to that Beauty which is the atmosphere and the real essence of the poem.

The Second Romantics

In the autumn of 1843, Baudelaire rented an apartment in the Hôtel Pimodan, an ancient building originally, and again today, known as the Hôtel Lauzun. The poet was young, rich, and popular and had before him every prospect of a splendid career. Théophile Gautier first met Baudelaire at the Hôtel Pimodan, through their mutual friend, the painter Fernand Boissard. Gautier tells us that Baudelaire, at the time, was still largely an undiscovered talent, preparing himself in the shadow for the light to come, with that tenacious power of will which, with him, doubled as inspiration; but his name was already known among the poets and artists, with a certain shiver of anticipation, and the younger generation expected much of him. Gautier adds that the poet's appearance was striking: his hair was close-cropped and jet black, curling in regular points over a starkly white forehead; his eyes were the color of Spanish tobacco, with a deep, spiritual gaze, and a penetration that was perhaps a bit too insistent. A silky mustache framed lips as sinuous and ironic as those painted by Leonardo da Vinci. His nose was fine and delicate; his neck, of a feminine elegance. He wore a jacket of the finest cloth, velvet black and lustrous, russet-brown pants, white socks, and patent shoes, the whole meticulously proper and correct, as if he wished to distinguish himself from those artists who favored soft felt hats and velvet vests. Gautier writes that his politeness was excessive, to the point of appearing mannered:

> He measured his phrases, employing only the most carefully chosen words, pronouncing them in a unique fashion, as if he wished to underline them and clothe them in an air of mysterious importance. He spoke in italics and capital letters. In contrast to the somewhat casual manner of most artists, he went to great lengths to uphold the strictest conventions. He would advance some satanically monstrous axiom or introduce a mathematical extravagance with an icy cool detachment. He established connections that the rest of us could only struggle to comprehend but which, nevertheless, struck us by their sense of bizarre logic. His gestures were slow, serious, and held close to the body, for he had a horror of Southern gesticulation. Nor did he care for verbal volubility—British reserve seemed to him the

height of good taste. One might say that he was a dandy who had strayed into Bohemia.

These strict rules of dress and conduct represented Baudelaire's ideal of effort and deliberation. The poet, it has been said, was so possessed of the absolute love of perfection that he applied himself with equal care to everything he did, and devoted as much minute attention to the polishing of his nails as to the writing of a sonnet! While resident in the Hôtel Pimodan it was, in the year 1844 or 1845, that Baudelaire first became acquainted with Théodore de Banville. In *Mes Souvenirs,* Banville describes the rooms where Baudelaire lived during what were, perhaps, the happiest years of his life:

> The poet lived then in the ancient and venerable Hôtel Pimodan, the decorative paintings of which have since been transferred to the Louvre. Those noble lodgings held apartments worthy of lords, notably those of the painter Boissard, who was enormously proud of his piano, and with reason, for it was painted entirely by the hand of Watteau! He had paid 1,200 francs for it, and today only a Rothschild could afford it. Baudelaire had chosen for himself a smaller apartment, with very high ceilings and a view of the wide green river. The wallpaper, patterned red and black, perfectly matched the antique Damask curtains that fell in heavy folds to the floor.

> The poet's majestic furniture included an immense table of walnut and several armchairs of oak, also of colossal proportions. A whole series of Delacroix's Hamlet lithographs, framed and behind glass, hung upon the walls. The two or three dozen of Baudelaire's volumes, chiefly the works of old French and Latin poets, occupied a simple cupboard. By an association of ideas only too natural, the magnificent books were casually stacked beside bottles of good Rhine wine.

In the month of December, Gautier walked through the rainy streets of Paris; it was six o'clock, perhaps, when he arrived at the Hôtel Pimodan:

I pulled vigorously at the carved bell until the door of massive wood rolled back upon its hinges. An old porter, framed in the trembling glow of a candle, appeared from behind a panel of yellowed glass. I passed through an archway into the courtyard which, as nearly as I could distinguish by the pale light that shed its lustre over the damp paving stones, seemed completely hemmed in by ancient buildings with tall pointed gables. My feet became as wet as if I had been walking across a lawn, for the interspaces of the stones were filled with grass. I entered the hall and at once noticed an immense staircase of the type that was built in the time of Louis XIV. An Egyptian chimera, sitting on a marble pedestal, gripped a candle in one of its claws. Paintings, copies of masterpieces of the Italian school, hung upon the walls of stone and wood. On the high ceilings were frescoes representing mythological scenes.

It was here, in the apartments of Boissard, that the Club des Hachichins gathered. "The room in which I found myself," Gautier continued, "was vast, and its decorations were profuse. The back portion alone was illuminated by the light of several suspended lamps. The walls, paneled woodwork painted white, were covered by antique paintings. A statue, which might have been removed from the leafy bowers of Versailles, stood atop an enormous oven. The ceiling, rounded into a cupola, was painted with allegorical figures in the style of Lemoine, and the work might indeed have been by his hand. At the back of the room I could distinguish, seated around the table, several human forms. They greeted me with loud cries as I stepped into the light. The doctor stood beside a buffet of oak, upon which rested a tray crowded with porcelain saucers. He offered to every guest, from a crystal glass, a small morsel of the Oriental hashish. Once each person had eaten his portion, coffee was served in the Arab manner, that is to say, with marc, and without sugar." Following a light dinner, each guest sat back to await at his leisure the first bouts of paradise.

In "The Poem of Hashish," Baudelaire describes how Balzac attended, one evening, a meeting of the club. The celebrated author of *Louis Lambert* handed back the potent herb without having tried it, for he scorned any substance that would sap his will. Balzac did, however, satisfy his curiosity on another occasion, as he confided to Madame de Hanska:

> I am resistant to hashish; my mind is too strong to be swayed and will not succumb to the drug's action. A greater quantity would have been necessary; and yet, I heard celestial choirs and saw divine paintings of surpassing beauty. I descended the stairway of the Lauzun [Hôtel Pimodan] for twenty years. The glimmer of the lamp flames and the lights of the drawing-room, the carving and gilding, all were embued with an inconceivable splendor. But this morning, since awakening, I have felt drowsy and completely drained of will.[5]

In *Les Paradis artificiels*, Baudelaire was chiefly concerned with portraying those modifications of human sentiment brought about by close association with the stimulant drugs; he sought to present the truths of medicine and science with the severest literalness, and without ornamentation. By contrast, Gautier's memorably beautiful narratives abound in splendid visions; the character of the hallucination impresses itself upon his writings,

---

5. Letter, 23 December 1845.

so that the forms and images of his reveries constitute a central object of attention:

> I was perfectly calm all through dinner, even while noticing that my companion's eyes had begun to strangely shine as they changed in color to a remarkable turquoise-blue. I was still in perfect possession of my senses. I went to sit on the divan, there to await ecstasy amidst the comfort of Moroccan pillows.
>
> Soon after, I fell into a state of heavy lethargy. My body seemed to dissolve until it became completely transparent. There was the hashish, glimmering with emerald fire inside my chest. My eyelashes lengthened immeasurably and wrapped, like gold threads, around a small ivory spindle which then began to spin with astonishing speed. Shimmering cascades of multicolored gemstones, arabesques and flowers presented themselves in endless succession, in effects which I can only compare to those of a kaleidoscope. I could still see my friends, but they were now transfigured, having assumed the forms of plants and beasts: here an ibis pensively standing on one foot, there an ostrich flapping its wings so bizarrely that I could not help but collapse with laughter in my corner. And, that I might more thoroughly participate in the festival, I launched my pillows into the air, catching each as it fell with the skill of a juggler.[6]

Origin, Growth, and Structure of Les Paradis artificiels

Having written "Du Vin and du hachish" in 1851, Baudelaire set about revising the section on hashish for republication in 1858.

---

6. "Le Hachich," *La Presse,* 10 July 1843.

It appeared in the *Revue contemporaine* in September of that year as "De l'Idéal artificiel—Le Haschisch." This later study became "Le Poëme du haschisch" in *Les Paradis artificiels*.

It was in the year 1857 that Baudelaire first spoke of joining, to his study on hashish, an article to be based upon Thomas De Quincey's *Confessions of an English Opium-Eater, Being an Extract From the Life of a Scholar*. De Quincey's work had been published anonymously in the *London Magazine* in September and October 1821, and appeared as a separate volume in 1822, with only minor revisions and the addition of an appendix. Immensely popular, the *Confessions* went through numerous reprintings with only slight modifications. The work was much enlarged and revised, however, in 1856. Baudelaire based his translation entirely on the original *Confessions*,[7] to which he added sections of De Quincey's sequel, the *Suspiria de Profundis*.

The *Suspiria*, originally conceived on a grand scale,[8] was abruptly broken off after just four installments in *Blackwood's* (that is, halfway through part 2). Finding it impossible to adhere to his plan, De Quincey published separately, as contributions to sundry periodicals, almost half of the thirty-two pieces he had intended to include in the *Suspiria*, with the rest being either thoroughly rewritten or lost.[9]

In *Les Paradis artificiels*, Baudelaire tells us that he first read the

---

7. With one exception: As De Quincey's comment on "keepsakes" appears only in the expanded edition, Baudelaire's reference to these lines in the "Preliminary Confessions" shows that he at least read the 1856 edition, even if he chose not to incorporate any other parts of it. Did he perhaps shrink from the labor of altering individual bits of information diffused so widely throughout the text?

8. The ambitious design of the *Suspiria* is briefly outlined in "Levana and Our Ladies of Sorrows."

9. For full information on this topic, see the *Posthumous Works of Thomas De Quincey*, edited by A. H. Japp (London, 1891).

Confessions before De Quincey had published their complement, the *Suspiria*, in 1845. This would most likely date his acquaint-ance with the *Confessions* to the epoch of the Hôtel Pimodan and the meetings of the Club des Hachichins.[10] By examining Baudelaire's correspondence, we can follow the work's genesis.

Baudelaire first spoke of the translation in a July 1857 letter to his mother: "The Opium-Eater is a new translation of a magnifi-cent author who is not yet known in Paris; it's for the *Moniteur*." In the eager confidence with which Baudelaire embarked on the project, he anticipated its swift completion. He sent the first chapters of the translation to the *Moniteur*'s director, Julien Turgan. "I will be sending you substantial packages on a daily basis," he told Turgan, "and I believe that all will be ready by the fifteenth."[11] But the offices of the *Moniteur* looked with horror upon the account of the opium eater. "The bizarre nature of the work frightens them," Baudelaire told his mother.[12] The *Moniteur* at length rejected the work and Baudelaire was forced to look elsewhere for a publisher.

Meanwhile, he had been engaged by the *Revue contemporaine* to write an article on hashish, which was to appear in the autumn of 1858. Finding no other outlet for his translation of the

---

10. It is worthwhile here to observe that De Quincey also wrote about hashish in his 1845 article "National Temperance Movements": "Now, I confess to having had a lurking insterest in this extract of hemp when I first heard of it; and at intervals a desire will continue to make itself felt for some deeper compression or centralization of the genial feelings than ordinary life affords. But old things will not avail; and new things I am now able to resist. Still, as the occasional craving does really arise in most men, it is well to notice it, and chiefly for the purpose of saying that this dangerous feeling wears off by degrees, and oftentimes for long periods it intermits so entirely as to be even displaced by a profound disgust to all modes of artificial stimulation."

11. Letter, 9 December 1857.

12. Letter, 13 May 1858.

Confessions, and badly in need of funds, Baudelaire offered this work, as well, to the review. The study on opium could thus logically follow the study on hashish. But the project, under the direction of Alphonse de Calonne, now changed form. Calonne refused to publish the complete work and told Baudelaire that he had to omit, for lack of room, various sections of the translation, which could be replaced by analysis and summary. To these demands the poet reluctantly agreed, but not without first voicing his objections:

> I assure you that confining the description of this complex book to such a SMALL space, while retaining every nuance, is not an easy task. This you will see. The extensive biographical details are not only amusing but are also most necessary, in that they serve as the key to *Opium's* highly personal dream visions.[13]

The unhappy poet was already a slave to opium, which he took in the form of laudanum. His confidence in the work, as year-end approached, had given way to doubt. His article on hashish had appeared as planned in September, but the work on opium was still far from completion. To his mother he wrote:

> My *Opium* causes me much distress; I have the idea that I've written something detestable. How dreadful to have gained an intimate knowledge of these poisons without having learned the means by which to extract more talent from them.[14]

The poet was now plagued by debt, which added to his distress. He decided to flee his creditors by removing himself to his mother's villa at Honfleur. To Calonne he said, "I fear that I shall be unable to deliver the final pages of my Opium-Eater

---

13. Letter to Alphonse de Calonne, 10 November 1858.
14. Letter, 11 December 1858.

anywhere else but there, in that small town of which I have spoken."[15] Madame Aupick, reluctant at first, finally agreed to her son's plans, but not before making him painfully aware of the many failings in his filial obligations.

The intricate arrangement of sentences favored by the English author were not easy to summarize. De Quincey's turn of mind was, to speak in the words of Coleridge, at once systematic and labyrinthine, and Baudelaire had the greatest difficulty bringing together the various windings of the narrative. The translation went through a variety of transformations until it finally became the "amalgam" of which the poet speaks in his letters:

> De Quincey is a frightfully conversational and digressive author. It is no small task to give this summary a dramatic form and to introduce order therein. Furthermore, I must fuse my personal feelings with those of the author to create an amalgam, the two halves of which must combine to form an indistinguishable whole. Have I succeeded?[16]

The director of the *Revue contemporaine* insisted that lack of space made the excision of even more material imperative, and the pressure of his complaints drove the poet to the point of distraction:

> My dear Calonne, I shall refuse for the first time. I am convinced that, from a literary viewpoint, I am in the right. You cause me even greater embarrassment than *astonishment*.
>
> The citations in question are of an immortal and unique beauty. Indeed, these citations (*the pains*) are an *indispensable* counterbalance to the citations that precede them (*the pleasures*).[17]

---

15. Letter, 8 January 1859.
16. Letter to Poulet-Malassis, 16 February 1860.
17. Letter to Alphonse de Calonne, 14 December 1859.

In the *Suspiria*, De Quincey narrated a succession of dream visions, in which, as he says, he examines his childhood at a distance of more than fifty years, through the powerful medium of opium. Baudelaire, having already laid the foundations of his translation of the *Confessions*, then decided to introduce extracts from this later work. He described his intentions in a letter to Calonne:

> Now I will say that there follows, after the morbid visions and the paradoxical method of the cure, a second part, mysterious and traversed by shadows, in which the reminiscences—not of youth but of childhood—are naturally transformed, are *opiated* by the imagination of a sixty-year-old man who has long been given to this strange habit.[18]

Soon afterward, Baudelaire struck upon an idea that lifted his spirits; he would transfer the famous lines of De Quincey "Oh! just, subtle, and mighty opium!" to the opening of the translation. "I have found at last," he told Calonne, "the beginning of the discourse, which resembles, in solemnity, the opening measures of an orchestra!"[19]

It was in the month of January that the *Opium-Eater* at last appeared in the *Revue contemporaine*. Baudelaire then began to revise the article, restoring the passages that had been cut by Calonne, in preparation for its publication, in combination with the study on hashish, as a separate volume. The dedication "To J.G.F." and the subtitles were introduced at this time. But the poet was apprehensive about the tone of his dedication, which he felt betrayed a profound contempt. As he told his mother, "It

---

18. Letter, December 1859.
19. Letter, 5 January 1860.

is so haughty, so full of insolence and scorn, that I vaguely feel as if I'm bordering on the ridiculous."[20]

The book had not yet been given a definite title. In a January letter to Poulet-Malassis, Baudelaire listed several possibilities, including *The Paradise of the Damned, The Pharmakon Nepenthes, The Lotus-Eaters,* and *Artificial Paradise,* at that date still in the singular. The subtitle, the poet stressed, should be "Hashish and Opium." The next month, *Les Paradis artificiels,* in the plural, was chosen as the title, with *Opium et haschisch* as the subtitle. The book went to press in March and reached the public in May. Baudelaire himself was more than satisfied with the result, as he told the publisher Michel Lévy in a letter of 1862: "My dear Michel, you must have the courage to read this from *beginning to end.* Keep this edition carefully, for you will see that it is very well done, and it will become impossible to find. There is *nothing to change,* the book is quite good as it is."

---

20 Letter, January 1860

On Wine and Hashish

Compared as Means
of Augmenting the Individuality
[1851]

I. WINE

A very famous man who was also a great fool, things that often seem to go hand in hand, as I will doubtlessly have the painful pleasure of proving more than once, dared to write, in a book on dining composed from the double viewpoint of diet and pleasure, the following in his entry on wine: "Father Noah, as old stories tell us, invented wine; it is a drink made from the fruit of the grapevine."

And then? After that, nothing at all: there is no more. You can skim the volume all you like, turn it over, read it forward and backward, from left to right and from right to left, and you will find nothing more about wine in *The Physiology of Taste* by the illustrious and much respected Brillat-Savarin than: "*Father Noah.* " and "it is a drink .."*

I imagine that an inhabitant of the moon or some other remote planet, traveling to our world and weary from his journey, would seek to slake his thirst and fill his stomach.* Having heard vague rumors of the delicious drinks that restore hope and courage to the people of this sphere, this traveler, that he might make an informed choice, consults the bible of taste, the famous, infallible Brillat-Savarin and, under the heading Wine, finds this precious information: "*Father Noah.. *" and "*this drink is made. *" That is indeed very helpful. Very enlightening. After reading this sentence, one could not help but have a correct and clear idea of all the wines, their unique characteristics, their disadvantages, and the powers they hold over the stomach and brain

Ah! dear friends, do not read Brillat-Savarin. *May God*

---

*Asterisks within the text refer to notes that will be found beginning on page 165. Daggers refer to Baudelaire's notes, which will be found at the foot of the page

preserve those he loves from useless reading; this is the first maxim in a little book by Lavater,* a philosopher who had more love for man than have all the magistrates of the modern and ancient worlds combined. No cakes have been named for Lavater; but the memory of that angelic man will live on among Christians long after the good bourgeois themselves have forgotten the Brillat-Savarin, a sort of tasteless brioche which serves, at best, as an excuse for the vomitings of inanely pedantic maxims taken from the famous masterpiece.

Drinkers doleful and merry, you who have sought in wine remembrance or forgetfulness and, always unfulfilled in this purpose, no longer gaze at the sky save through the bottom of a bottle,† drinkers forsaken and misunderstood, if a new edition of this pseudo-masterpiece dares to insult the common sense of modern man, are you going to buy a copy and so exchange good for bad and kindness for indifference?

I open the *Kreisleriana*, by the divine Hoffmann*, and my gaze falls upon a curious recommendation. The conscientious musician must drink champagne before composing a comic opera: he finds in his glass all of the bubbling joy for which the genre is known. Religious music must be accompanied by Rhine or Jurançon wine. As from the depths of profound thought, an inebriating bitterness is found therein. But for a march of glory there must be Burgundy, in which the music of patriotic passion burns. Here surely is something of higher worth and, aside from the ardent expressions of a dedicated drinker, I find in this work an impartiality that does a German the greatest honor.

Hoffmann developed a unique psychological barometer which allowed him to observe the varying temperatures and atmospheric phenomena of his soul. Thus we find such divisions as these: "vaguely ironic mood tempered with indulgence; desire for

---

†Béroalde de Verville, *Le Moyen de parvenir.* *

solitude and feelings of deep self-contentment; musical joy, musical enthusiasm, musical tempest; sarcastic gaiety, which even I cannot tolerate, profound desire to quit my *self*, excessive objectivity; fusion of my being with nature."

Needless to say, the divisions of Hoffmann's moral barometer were established according to the sequence in which they were generated, as are those of an ordinary barometer. There appears to be an obvious bond between this psychic barometer and the explanation of wine's musical qualities.

Hoffmann's finances were just beginning to improve at the moment that death came to claim him. Fortune smiled on him. The same was true with our great beloved Balzac, who saw the aurora borealis of his brightest hopes only as he neared his final hour. The directors of newspapers and reviews, clamoring for contributions from his pen, then sent him, to win his favor, cases of French wine along with their monetary dispatches.

II

What man has never known the profound joys of wine? Whoever has had a grief to appease, a memory to evoke, a sorrow to drown, a castle in Spain to build—all have at one time invoked the mysterious god who lies concealed in the fibers of the grapevine. How radiant are those wine-induced visions, brilliantly illuminated by the inner sun! How true and burning this second youth which man draws from wine. But how dangerous, too, are its fierce pleasures and debilitating enchantments. And so I ask the judges, legislators, and worldly men, all of you on whom good fortune smiles, to tell us truly: Would you, in your soul and conscience, have the pitiless courage to condemn a man who drinks of genius?

To be sure, wine is not always a terrible adversary sure of victory, sworn to show neither pity nor mercy. Wine is like man:

you can never be sure how much it should be esteemed or scorned, loved or hated, nor of how many sublime deeds or monstrous deceits it is capable. Thus we should not view it more harshly than we view ourselves. Let us treat wine as our equal.

I sometimes imagine that I can hear the voice of wine.* It speaks from its soul in a low musical language that only the spirit can understand: "Man, my dear friend, despite my glass prison bolted with cork, I wish to sing you a song of true fraternity, a song that is merry, full of light and hope. I am not ungrateful, I know that I owe you my life. I know the pain your labors cost you, with the bright sun beating down on your shoulders. You have given me life, for which I will abundantly reward you. I will generously repay my debt, for I feel great joy when I fall down a throat parched by toil. I would sooner dwell in the stomach of an honest man, a cheerful grave wherein I enthusiastically fulfill my destiny, than in these dreary, unfeeling cellars. I raise a mighty turbulence within the laborer's stomach and from there mount up invisible ladders into the brain, where I execute my supreme dance.

"Can you hear the powerful refrains of ancient times, the songs of love and glory, resounding and echoing within me? I am the soul of your native land, half soldier and half gentleman. I am Sunday's hope. As *work makes for prosperous days*, so wine makes for joyful Sundays. Pay me proud tribute, with your shirtsleeves rolled back and your elbows leaning upon the family table, and you shall know true contentment.

"I will brighten the eye of your old wife, partner of your daily sorrows and of your brightest hopes. I will soften her gaze and restore the youthful glow to her eye. And your dear son, the pale little donkey, as saddled with worries as a dray horse, for him I will be as the oil that anointed the limbs of wrestlers in ancient days.

"I will drop into your chest like a vegetal ambrosia. I will be the grain that regenerates the cruelly plowed furrow. Poetry will be born of our intimate union. A God we shall create together, and we shall soar heavenward like sunbeams, perfumes, butterflies, birds, and all winged things."

Thus sings wine in its mysterious language. Woe to him whose egotistical heart is closed to his brother's misfortunes, having never heard this song!

I suppose that if Jesus Christ were called before a tribunal today, a prosecutor would claim that recidivism had aggravated his case. But wine is a beneficial recidivist; it restores us daily and daily delivers new blessings. This doubtlessly explains the moralist's animosity toward it. When I say moralist, I mean the pseudo-moralist hypocrite.

But there is much more. Let us now delve deeper. Let us observe one of those mysterious souls who earns his living, so to speak, on the refuse of large cities. For such unusual labors do exist, and in great number. I have sometimes thought with horror that there were labors that brought no joy, labors that brought no pleasure, worries without comfort, sorrows without recompense. There I was wrong. This man is responsible for gathering up the daily debris of the capital. All that the city has rejected, all it has lost, shunned, disdained, broken, this man catalogs and stores. He sifts through the archives of debauch, the junkyards of scrap. He creates order, makes an intelligent choice; like a miser hoarding treasure, he gathers the refuse that has been spit out by the god of Industry, to make of it objects of delight or utility. By the somber red glow of street lamps battered by storm and night,* this man climbs the long meandering streets that run past rows of neat houses along Sainte-Geneviève Hill. He is equipped with his willow basket and staff. He proceeds, shaking his head and stumbling over the cobblestones like the young poets who spend their days wandering in search of rhymes. He talks to himself, pouring out his soul to the cold night shadows. His monologue is splendid enough to shame even the most lyrical of tragedies. "Forward, march! Company, about-face! Present arms!" Exactly like Napoleon agonizing at Saint Helena! His staff has become an iron sceptre and his willow basket an imperial cloak. He congratulates his army. The battle is won but the day has been difficult. He passes on horseback beneath triumphal arches. His heart is glad. He listens ecstatically to the cheers of an admiring crowd. Soon he will draw up some mightier law than ever has man proclaimed. He solemnly swears to please his people. Never again shall misery and vice plague human hearts.

And yet his back and thighs are scraped raw by the weight of his basket. He is tormented by the cares of life. He is exhausted by the unceasing toil of forty years. Age lies heavily upon him. But wine, like a new Pactolus,* rolls a sympathetic gold over languishing humanity. Like the good kings, wine reigns through benevolence and sings its exploits in the throats of its subjects.

There are on this planet innumerable, unnamed masses of people who, even in the calm of sleep, can find no respite from their sorrow. For them, wine composes songs and poems.

I am sure that many readers will undoubtedly deem me too indulgent. "You justify drunkenness, you idealize debauchery." I must admit that in the face of wine's powerful merits, I do not have the courage to dwell on its faults. Indeed, I have already said that wine and man are strongly allied, and I have conceded that the crimes of each are equal to their virtues. Can I do better? I have, in any event, another idea. If the production of wine were ever to cease, its absence would create a void, a vacuum more terrible than all of the excesses and offenses for which it is blamed. Is it not reasonable to believe that people who never drink wine are either idiots or hypocrites: idiots, that is to say, those who know nothing of humanity and nature, artists who disdain the traditional means of art; workers who curse the machinery; and hypocrites, that is to say, the shameful gluttons, the flag wavers of sobriety who drink in secret from some carefully concealed bottle? A man who drinks only water has a secret to keep from his peers.

Let us consider further: Some years ago, at an art exhibit, I observed a crowd of imbeciles standing agape before a painting that was as highly polished, waxed, and varnished as an industrial object. The work was the absolute antithesis of art. It was, to Drölling's *Cuisine,** what madness is to foolishness, and what a man of fanatic devotion is to a follower. In that microscopic painting could be seen flies in flight. I, too, was drawn toward that monstrous object; but I felt ashamed of this pecular weakness, for it was the irresistible attraction to the horrible. At length, I realized that I had been unwittingly moved by a philosophic curiosity. I longed to discover the moral character of the man who had dared to bring forth such a criminal extravagance. He must be corrupt, I wagered with myself, positively corrupt. My instinct delighted in winning this psychological wager. Having made some inquiries about him, I found that the monster rose regularly before dawn and *drank only milk!*

One or two more stories before we take a stand. One day, I noticed a throng of people gathered on the sidewalk; I managed to raise my eyes above the bystanders' shoulders, and saw this scene: A man lay upon his back on the ground, stretched full length. His eyes were open, gazing upward at the sky. By his side there stood another man, who spoke to him through gestures; the man on the ground replied with his eyes only, and the two of them were animated by an air of extraordinary goodwill. The standing man's gestures spoke silently to his companion: "Rise up, friend, and stand by me; happiness awaits us at the corner, just two steps away. The shores of sorrow are not yet out of sight, nor have we yet reached the *high seas* of dream. Have courage, my friend, and let us walk on. Bid your legs to do your will!"

All of this was accompanied by much swaying and harmonious balancing. The other man had obviously already reached the *high seas* (he was, indeed, navigating in the gutter), for his blissful smile replied: "Leave your friend in peace. A charitable mist conceals the banks of sorrow; I have nothing more to ask of the heavens than that I be left to dream." And at length his voice was heard in a vaguely whispered phrase or rather the hint of a sigh that formed the words: "Be reasonable!" This scene reaches the very *ne plus ultra* of sublimity, and yet there is a hypersublimity in inebriation, as we shall see. The friend, still indulgent, went on to the tavern alone, only to return moments later holding a rope in his hand. Apparently, he could not resign himself to the idea of looking for happiness on his own, which was why he came to collect his friend in a carriage. The carriage was the strong rope, which he then carefully fastened around his friend's waist. The man on the ground smiled, for he clearly understood this maternal gesture. The other man tied a knot; then set off at a trot like a docile horse. And so they proceeded, the man who was being carted, or rather dragged, polished the pavement as he went, all the while beaming with an ineffable smile, until they reached the very door to happiness.

The crowd was awed; for that which is too beautiful, that which surpasses man's power of poetic expression, is often a source more of astonishment than of compassion.

There was a Spaniard, a guitarist, who traveled for many years with Paganini. This was before the epoch of Paganini's great rise to official glory.

The two of them led the vagabond life of bohemians, of wandering musicians, of people without ties to family or homeland. Together, guitar and violin, they gave concerts in every town and village through which they passed. And thus they wandered from country to country. This Spaniard's talent was so vast that he, like Orpheus, could say, "I am the master of Nature."

Everywhere he went, strumming his strings, making them sing harmoniously beneath his thumb, a crowd always followed. With such a secret, one never goes hungry. They followed him as Jesus Christ was followed. Who could refuse dinner and hospitality to this man, a genius, a sorcerer who had touched the depths of your soul with his most beautiful, most secret, most mysterious songs! This man, I am told, could easily obtain simultaneous sound from an instrument capable of yielding only a succession of notes. Paganini carried their money, and managed their budget, which ought not to surprise anybody.

The purse traveled on the administrator's person; sometimes up, sometimes down, today in the boots, tomorrow in the jacket lining. When the guitarist, who was fond of drink, asked what cash they had in coffer, Paganini replied that they were broke, or at least almost broke; for Paganini in this was like an elderly man, always afraid of being *in need*. The Spaniard believed him, or pretended to, and, his eyes fixed on the distant horizon, he harassed and tormented his inseparable companion. Paganini and the guitarist walked on opposite sides of the road; in this way, they could avoid arguments and study as they walked.

When they arrived in a town that seemed to offer some promise of profit, one of the two would play a tune of his own composition while the other, standing alongside him, improvised a melody, a countermelody, a variation. No one can guess the pleasure and poetry they found in their troubadour existence. They separated, for what reason I do not know. The Spaniard traveled alone. One evening, he arrived at a small town in the Jura, where he announced that he would be giving a concert at the town hall; *he* himself would be the concert, alone with his guitar. He made himself known, strumming in all of the taverns of the town. The local musicians were struck by his unique talent, and throngs of people came to hear him.

Our Spaniard encountered another Spaniard, a *countryman*, in a section of the town near the cemetery. He was a sort of graveyard contractor, a marblecutter who fashioned tombstones.

Like most men in the funeral trades, he was a dedicated drinker. So it was that the bottle and their common homeland carried them a long way together; the musician never left the marblecutter's side. On the very day of the concert, the hour the guitarist was to play, they were still together, but where? The musician had to be found. All of the taverns and cafés were searched. He was finally unearthed with his friend, in an unspeakable dive, both of them beastly drunk. There ensued performances to rival those of Frédérick and Kean.* He at last agreed to play; but then an idea suddenly occurred to him: "You will accompany me." His friend refused; he owned a violin, but played as badly as the worst street fiddler. "If you won't play, then neither will I."

Sermons and good sense failed to make an impression; there was nothing else for it—he had to give in. So there they stood upon the stage, before the town's best bourgeoisie. "Fetch me wine!" cried the Spaniard. The marblecutter, whom everyone knew, though not as a musician, was too far gone to feel ashamed. The wine brought, the two scoundrels were so impatient to open the bottles that, like men of low breeding, they cut open the corks with stabs of their knives. You can imagine the wonderful effect this had on the provincials dressed in all their finery! The ladies walked out and much of the audience, scandalized by the spectacle of these two seemingly mad drunkards, exited the hall.

But how richly rewarded were those who allowed curiosity to triumph over propriety, those who were courageous enough to stay. "Begin," commanded the guitarist. It is impossible to convey the precise nature of the sounds that rose from the drunken violin, sounds resembling those of a delirious Bacchus, perhaps, cutting stone with a saw? What was he playing, or trying to play? No matter, the first melody had begun. Suddenly, a tune alternately energetic, subtle, and capricious, smothered and extinguished the jarring din. The guitar sang ever louder until it overwhelmed the violin; and yet, here was the same melody, the same vinous air that the marblecutter had begun.

The guitar held forth with enormous sonority; it cried, sang, and declamed with an astounding liveliness, and a surety, an inexpressible purity of diction. The guitar improvised a variation on the blind violin's theme. The violin was guided by the guitar, which maternally clothed the frail nudity of its sound. Reader, you must understand that such a scene defies description. I heard this story from an eyewitness, a man of scrupulous integrity. In the end, the audience was more drunk than the musician. The Spaniard was cheered, congratulated, and celebrated with enormous enthusiasm. But the character of the townspeople apparently displeased him, for he never agreed to play there again.

And where is he now? What sun looks down upon his final dreams? What earth holds his cosmopolitan remains? What ditch harbors his last agony? Whither is fled the perfume of vanished flowers? Where are the enchanting lights of bygone setting suns?

III

Now certainly, I have not told you anything very new. Wine is known to all, admired by all. One day a truly philosophical physician—something that is rarely seen—will write an authoritative study on wine, a kind of double psychological profile in which wine and man make up the two subjects. He will explain how and why certain beverages immeasurably augment the personality of the thinking being and create, as it were, a third person through a mystical operation whereby natural man and wine, the animal god and the vegetal god, representing the Father and Son of the Trinity, combine to engender a Holy Ghost, the superior man, who proceeds equally from the two.

The restorative benefits of wine course so powerfully through the veins of some people that their legs become stronger and their sense of hearing becomes excessively acute. I knew of one individual who found that when he was drunk, his feeble eyesight fully regained its original, penetrating powers. Wine made an eagle of the mole.

As an unknown author once expressed it: "Nothing equals the joy of a man who drinks, unless it be the joy of the wine being drunk." To be sure, wine and man are intimately allied—so intimately, in fact, that I am not surprised to learn that some reasonable souls, seduced by the idea of pantheism, endow wine with a sort of personality. Wine and man are like two friends who follow every argument with a reconciliation; the winner always embraces the loser.

There are disagreeable drunkards; these are people who are naturally disagreeable. The bad individual become execrable, as the good becomes excellent.

I shall soon speak of a substance which has been fashionable now for several years, a delicious type of drug which is favored by a certain class of dilettante, on whom it acts with effects which are just as explosive as those of wine, although of an entirely different nature. I will carefully delineate its actions and, again illustrating the varying efficacies of wine, I will compare these two artificial means by which man provokes his personality, so to speak, into creating a sort of divinity within himself.

I will illustrate the disadvantages of hashish, not the least of which is its antisocial nature, in spite of the treasures of incomparable benevolence it seems to sow in man's heart, or rather brain, in contrast to wine, which is profoundly human and, I almost venture to say, tantamount to a man of action.

IV. HASHISH

When hemp is harvested, the gatherers, both male and female, at times experience certain strange phenomena. They say that a curious species of vertiginous spirit rises up from the crops to circle around their legs before mounting up maliciously to the brain. The harvester's head begins to spin, becomes heavy and charged with dreams. The limbs grow weak and refuse to serve. I can assure you that this is so, for I myself experienced similar phenomena when, as a child, I rolled among stacks of cut alfalfa.

Although there have been attempts to make hashish from French hemp, these efforts have, to date, entirely failed. The enthusiasts who would procure the magical delights of this substance at any price have continued to seek out hashish which has crossed the Mediterranean—that is, hashish made from Indian or Egyptian hemp. The compound of hashish is prepared from a decoction of Indian hemp, butter, and a small quantity of opium.

We have before us a morsel of uniquely scented green paste; its smell, indeed, is so powerful that it gives rise to a certain revulsion as do, for that matter, all fine scents when concentrated to their maximum strength and, so to speak, density. Take a spoonful, a portion the size of a nut, and happiness is yours; absolute happiness, with all of its exquisite pleasure, all of its youthful folly, all of its infinite rapture. Happiness is yours, in the form of a small bit of paste. Take it, have no fear, you will not die of it; your internal organs will not be harmed. It may, perhaps, weaken your resolve, but that is another matter.

Generally, for the hashish to reach its full potency and force, it must be taken on an empty stomach, dissolved in a cup of very hot black coffee. Dinner must be missed or at least delayed until ten o'clock or midnight; then a very light soup alone is tolerable. Infraction of this most simple rule will either cause vomiting, as the drug and the meal vie with each other, or will render the hasish ineffective. When this happens, many novices and imbeciles accuse the drug of lacking power.

As soon as the substance has been absorbed—an operation

which requires some resolution of will for, as I have said, the mixture's smell is so powerful that it can cause bouts of nausea in some people—you find yourself suddenly gripped by a certain inexplicable anxiety. You have heard the many vague rumors of the marvelous effects of hashish, your imagination has formed an image of the ideal intoxication, and you are burning to know if the reality will measure up to your expectations. The length of time between the absorption of the drug and the onset of the first symptoms will vary according to individual temperament and habit. People who are acquainted with hashish will frequently begin to experience, after half an hour, the first symptoms of the invasion.

I neglected to mention that, as hashish will heighten a man's personality while at the same time acutely sharpening his senses, it is advisable to yield to its influence only in the most favorable circumstances and in pleasant surroundings. Every delight, every contentment is magnified, and every pain, every anguish, is intensely and sharply felt. Do not dare venture such an experience if you have some disagreeable business to conclude, if your mood is exceptionally dark, or if you have bills to pay. As I have said, hashish renders a man incapable of action. It possesses none of the consoling benefits of wine; its only action is to immeasurably expand the human personality, within the circumstances in which it is placed. You should, as far as possible, arrange to be in an attractive apartment or a landscape-garden, with a few accomplices whose intellectual temperaments are similar to your own. Your mind should be clear and calm. A little music, too, is desirable.

At their first initiation, novitiates frequently complain that the drug is too slow to act. Impatiently awaiting its first effects, they utter cries of incredulity when these effects fail to appear quickly enough, much to the delight of those who are acquainted with the ways in which hashish manifests its presence. It is most amusing to see the first symptoms appear and multiply in the very midst of this incredulity. At first you are seized by an irresistible, ridiculous joy. The most common words, the simplest ideas, take on a bizarre, new meaning. This merriment is more than you can bear, but all efforts to resist it will prove to be futile. The demon has invaded you, and any struggle you mount will only serve to accelerate the progress of the affliction. You laugh at your idiocy and madness. Your friends, also, laugh at you, but you make no attempt to stop them. A gentle benevolence has now seized your spirit.

This languid merriment, this anxious delight, this insecurity and indecision which has been induced by the malady, lasts but for a short time. It sometimes happens that people thoroughly inept at word plays improvise interminable strings of puns, connect completely unrelated ideas, and dream up such deeds as to perplex even the strongest masters of this absurd art. Several moments later, the bonds of unison between your ideas grow so vague and frail, the thread that ties your conceptions so tenuous, that only your accomplices, your coreligionists can understand you. Your demonstrations of giddy cheer and uncontrolled laughter seem like the height of madness to the man who does not share your condition.

The prudence of this unfortunate soul cheers you immeasurably, his detachment pushes you beyond the limits of irony; he seems to you to be the maddest, the most absurd of men. As for your comrades, you understand them perfectly, and soon engage them in mute dialogues. Here, then, we have a comical situation, as you delight in sensations of rapture that are incomprehensible to those who are outside of your world. They are regarded with the profoundest pity. From this moment, the idea of your superiority dawns on your mind's horizon, soon to expand immeasurably.

Now, as to this first stage, I once witnessed two scenes of a strangely grotesque nature. A celebrated musician, who knew nothing experimentally of hashish and who, perhaps, knew it not even by name, arrived in the midst of a party where almost everyone was under its sway. They tried to convey to him something of its marvelous effects. He laughed gracefully like a man willing to be *tolerant* for a few moments, because he was polite. They all laughed, because those whose senses have yielded to hashish are, in this first stage, endowed with a marvelous comic sense. The wild demonstrations of joy, the incomprehensible outrages, the unfathomable puns, the baroque gestures, all continued. The musician declared that this extravagance could not be good for an artist and that it must, moreover, be quite exhausting for all involved.

The joy redoubled. "This extravagance may be good for you, but it doesn't suit me in the least," he said. "It suits us, that's all that matters," one of the afflicted egotistically replied. Bursts of idiotic laughter filled the room. Our man was offended and wished to leave, but the door was locked and someone had removed the key. Another man dropped to one knee before the musician, tearfully declaring that all of the present company felt the deepest pity for him, despite his inferiority.

They begged him to play and he reluctantly agreed. Scarcely had the first note sounded when the tones of the violin spread throughout the room, gripping first one, then another of the afflicted. So charged did the atmosphere become with sobs and sighs, rending cries and torrents of tears, that the frightened musician, thinking he was in a madhouse, set down his instrument. He approached the man who seemed most caught in the grips of the blissful tremors and asked him if he was suffering much, and if so, what might best be done to ease the pain. Another helpful soul, who had also refrained from tasting the beatific drug, suggested soda and bitters. The afflicted man, his eyes brimming over with ecstasy, looked at him with unutterable scorn; only pride saved him from taking serious offense. Indeed, what is more likely to offend an enraptured man than the suggestion that he be cured of his bliss?

Here we have a curious phenomenon: a servant was sent to buy tobacco and refreshments for a gathering at which everyone had taken hashish. When she returned, she found herself surrounded by bizarre heads with staring eyes. Then, as if enslaved by that malevolent atmosphere of collective madness, she uttered a wild laugh and fled panic-stricken from the room. The next day she explained that, for a duration of several hours, she had been subject to the most extraordinary sensations. The feeling had been very odd, she said, and was totally different from any she had experienced before; and yet, she had not used hashish.

The second stage is heralded by a feeling of coldness in the extremities and a vague oppression which seizes your drowsed senses; your fingers turn, as they say, to butter. Your head grows heavy and a general numbness pervades your entire being. Your eyes grow abnormally large, as if pulled by an implacable ecstasy; your countenance pales, turns livid and green. Your lips recede and retract, seeming to disappear within your mouth. Deep, hoarse sighs escape your chest, as if your old nature could not bear the weight of your new nature. Your senses become extraordinarily acute. Your eyes pierce the infinite. Your ears clearly distinguish the slightest sounds amid the most discordant din.

Then the hallucinations begin. External things, forms and images, swell to monstrous proportions, revealing themselves in fantastic shapes as yet unimagined. Instantly passing through a variety of transformations, they enter your being, or rather you enter theirs. The most singular ambiguities, the most inexplicable transpositions of ideas take place in your sensations. Sound holds color, color holds music.* Musical notes become numbers and you resolve, with astonishing rapidity, prodigious arithmetical calculations in time to the music that swells in your ears. You are seated, smoking a pipe; you think that you are sitting inside the pipe, but the pipe, rather, is smoking you; you exhale yourself in spirals of blue clouds.

You feel fine, but your mind is obsessed by this one thought: How will you get out of your pipe? These fancies last an eternity. An interval of lucidity allows you to glance, though not without great effort, at the clock: Eternity has lasted for exactly one minute. You are then borne off on another current, which holds you in the wave of its living whirlpool, and this moment, too, seems to last an eternity. The proportions of time and existence are distorted by the crowded confusion of your feelings and the intensity of your ideas. You live several lifetimes in the space of an hour. Clearly, this is the subject of *La Peau de chagrin.** The accord between the senses and their pleasures is broken. The individual's conscious nature disappears from time to time. Objectivity, which has produced a number of pantheistic poets and all of the great actors, assumes such force that your confused perceptions cannot distinguish your own being from that of others. You are the tree that sighs in the wind singing to nature vegetal melodies. Now you soar in azure heavens grown immense. Grief has vanished. You are borne off without a struggle; you have suffered the loss of self-command, but this you cannot regret. Soon the idea of time will completely vanish. Brief spells of lucidity still occur at intervals; you seem then to have left a marvelous, fantastic world. True, you still possess the faculty of self-observation, and tomorrow you will have retained the memory of your sensations. But the ability to apply this psychological faculty will be beyond your reach. I defy you to sharpen either pencil or quill; these actions would be beyond your capabilities.   *

At other times, music recites you infinite poems, or places you within frightening or fantastic dramas. Harmony and melody

become inextricably linked with the objects around you. Paintings upon the ceiling, even the most mediocre or dismal, take on
a startling life of their own. A limpid, enchanting river winds
through a field of trembling flowers. Nymphs with gleaming skin
gaze at you with immense eyes clearer than water or sky. You take
your place and play your part in the most wretched paintings, in
the coarsest scenes painted on the walls of the most common
inn's rooms.

I have before suggested that, for those who are artistically
inclined, water takes on a disturbing charm when illuminated by
hashish. Waterfalls, babbling jets of water, harmonious cascades,
and the blue expanses of the sea will sing, flow, and sleep in the
innermost depths of your mind. It would be, perhaps, less than
wise to permit a man in such a condition to linger on the banks
of some still pool; like the fisherman in the ballad, he might
allow himself to be carried off by the undine.

Toward the end of the evening you might venture a light meal,
but this operation is not easily accomplished. You are so far above
the material world that you would certainly prefer to linger in the
depths of your intellectual paradise. It sometimes happens, however, that a voracious hunger develops in an extraordinary way; and
yet great courage is needed simply to lift a bottle, fork, or knife.

The third stage, separated from the second by a redoubling of
the crisis, a dizzying intoxication followed by a new bout of
uneasiness, is something which defies description. It is what
Orientals term *kef*, the state of perfect bliss. No longer do storms
and tempests trouble your senses; this is a calm, immobile
happiness. All philosophical problems are resolved. All of the
secrets about which theologians have grappled and which have
been the despair of human understanding, now appear transparent and clear. All contradiction is resolved. *Man becomes god.*

There is a voice within you that says: "You are superior to all
humanity, no one understands what you are thinking, what you

are experiencing at this moment. They could not even begin to understand the great love you feel for them. But they should be pitied for this, not despised. Immense vistas of happiness and virtue stretch before you. No one can imagine the extent of your virtue or the power of your intellect. Live within your solitary thoughts and avoid distressing your fellow man."

You will experience, as one of the more grotesque effects of hashish, the fear of causing any human being the least pain or mortification—a fear which is pushed to a madness of meticulous extremes. You would even disguise, if you could, the exalted state you are in, to avoid causing the slightest offense.

For the gentle, artistic soul in this supreme state, love assumes the most unusual forms and lends itself to the most startlingly baroque combinations. A wild lustiness may mingle with tender, gentle, paternalistic sentiments.

My final observation will not be the least curious. When the first rays of daylight enter your room, your first sensation is one of profound astonishment. Time stands fixed. A moment ago it was night, now it is day. "Have I slept? Have I spent all night in an intoxicated slumber that surpressed the notion of time, so that the entire night seemed to have passed in the space of a second? Or rather was I caught in the veil of a sleep crowded with visions?" This is a matter which cannot be determined.

You seem to be endowed with a marvelous lightness and sense of well-being; you are not the least bit tired. But no sooner have you risen to your feet than a new bout of intoxication grips you. Your enfeebled legs carry you timidly and you are afraid that, should you fall, you would shatter like some fragile object. A vast languor, not without charm, settles over your mind, an indolence which prevents you from endeavoring any intellecual labor or action.

This is the punishment you deserve for having so carelessly, and with such impious prodigality, spent your vital energies. Your personality, which you have cast to the four winds, can only be regained by the greatest efforts of will.

V

I am not asserting that hashish produces in all men all of the effects that I have described here. I have more or less recounted the phenomena generally produced, except for a few variations, among individuals of artistic and philosophical bent. But there are others in whom the drug raises only a raucous madness, a violent merriment resembling vertigo, which brings on dancing, jumping and wild laughter. These individuals have, so to speak, a completely physical hashish. They are intolerable to the spiritualists, who profoundly pity them. Their vile personalities can give rise to scandal. I once saw a respectable judge—an honorable man, as society people are fond of saying, one of those men who clothe themselves in artificial seriousness—suddenly launch into the most indecent *cancan* as soon as the hashish invaded him. Thus is the interior, truthful monster awakened. This man who judged the actions of his peers, this *Solon*, had secretly learned to dance the cancan.

Hence it appears that this impersonality of which I have spoken, this objectivity, which is nothing more than the extreme development of the poetic mind, is never found in the hashish of these aforementioned types.

VI

In Egypt, the government prohibits the sale and trade of hashish, at least within the country's own borders. The poor souls who have succumbed to this passion visit the pharmacist under the pretext of purchasing another medication in order to collect their small quantity of hashish, which has been prepared for them in advance. The Egyptian government is correct in its reasoning. Never could a sane state survive with its people using hashish. It produces neither good soldiers nor good citizens. Clearly, man is forbidden, under penalty of ruin and intellectual decline, to disrupt the primordial conditions of his existence, to disturb the equilibrium between his faculties and his surroundings. If ever a government wished to corrupt its citizens, it would only have to encourage the use of hashish.

It is believed that hashish causes no physical harm; this is true enough, or at least no harm that has yet been recorded. For I am not sure to what extent we can say that a man is in perfect possession of his health when he is so far intoxicated as to be incapable of action, when he can do nothing but dream. For it is the human will, of all faculties the most precious, that is attacked. A man who could instantaneously attain all of the riches of heaven and earth by swallowing a spoonful of paste would never acquire the thousandth part by his own labors. One must, above all, live and work.

It occurred to me to speak of wine and hashish in the same article because, indeed, they have something in common: the extraordinary amplification of man's poetic nature. Man, in all ages, has shown a frantic taste for all substances, benign or dangerous, which exalt his personality and testify to his grandeur. He has always sought to revive his hopes and he has always yearned for the infinite. But the consequences must be considered. On the one hand we have a drink that stimulates the digestion, fortifies the muscles, and enriches the blood. Even taken in great quantities, it will cause only slight disturbances. On the other hand we have a substance that troubles the digestion, weakens the physical constitution, and may produce an intoxication that lasts up to twenty-four hours. Wine exalts the will, hashish destroys it. Wine is physically beneficial, hashish is a suicidal weapon. Wine encourages benevolence and sociability. Hashish isolates. One is industrious, in a manner of speaking, the other essentially indolent. What, indeed, is the use of working, laboring, writing, producing anything whatsoever, when paradise might be attained without the least effort? Finally, wine is for those people engaged in honest labor, those who are worthy of drinking it. Hashish is among the solitary pleasures, and is favored by miserable idlers. Wine is useful and produces fruitful results; hashish is useless and dangerous.†

VII

I close this article with the comment of a remarkable, little-known philosopher named Barbereau,* a musical theoretician and professor at the Conservatory. Seated next to him at a gathering at which several people had taken the enchanting poison, he said to me, with a tone of ineffable scorn: "I fail to understand why rational, reasoning man must employ artificial means to reach poetic bliss when he can, with enthusiasm and will, raise himself up to a supranatural existence.

"The great poets, philosophers, and prophets have all, by the free and pure exercise of their will, succeeded in reaching a state in which they were at once cause and effect, subject and object, mesmerizer and somnambulist."

There I completely agree.

---

†One need only mention here, for the record, the recent attempt to administer hashish as a cure for madness. The madman who takes hashish contracts a new madness that chases the first and, when the intoxication has passed, the true madness, which is the madman's normal state, regains ascendancy, in the same way that we regain our reason and health. Someone has taken the trouble to write a book on the subject. The doctor* who has invented this lovely system does not in the least belong to the philosophical world.

Artificial Paradises

Opium and Hashish

My Dear,

Good sense tells us that earthly things are rare and fleeting, and that true reality exists only in dreams. To draw sustenance from happiness—natural or artificial—you must first have the courage to swallow it; and those who perhaps most merit happiness are precisely those on whom felicity, as mortals conceive it, always acts as a vomitive.

Simple souls will find it unusual or even inappropriate that a portrayal of artificial pleasures should be dedicated to a woman, the most common source of the most natural pleasures. And further, it is evident that even as the natural world penetrates the spiritual and serves as its fodder, thus together moving to bring about that indefinable amalgam we call our individuality, so it is she who throws the strongest light or deepest shadows in our dreams. Woman is inevitably suggestive; she lives from a life other than her own; she lives spiritually in the imagination, which she haunts and nourishes.

I care little or nothing whether this dedication is understood. And, moreover, is it necessary to an author's satisfaction that a book such as this be understood, except by those for whom it is written? Must it have been written for someone? But I myself have so little love for the world of the living that—like those idle, sensitive women who are said to post letters to imaginary friends—I would gladly write only for the dead. And yet she to whom I dedicate this little book is not dead; she is, though ill, still active and living within me, her gaze upturned to Heaven, place of all transfigurations. For only man enjoys the privilege of drawing as much new and subtle pleasure from pain, suffering, and disaster as he does from a potent drug.

You will see in this picture a lone, melancholy man who wanders,* who plunges into the perpetual flow of the multitudes. He sends his heart and thoughts to a distant Electra, she who once wiped away the sweat from his forehead and refreshed his lips when they were parched with fever. And you will perceive the gratitude of another Orestes, you who so often bore him company through the heavy watches of the night and who banished his troubled slumber with a gentle, maternal hand.

C.B.

The Poem of Hashish

I. A TASTE FOR THE INFINITE

Every man who knows how to observe the capacities of his own intellect and who can retain the memory of his impressions, every man who, like Hoffmann,* can construct his own spiritual barometer—will at times have had occasion to remark, in the observatory of his thoughts, fair seasons, delightful days, and joyful minutes. There are days when a man awakens with a young, vigorous genius. Scarcely has he cleared the sleep from his eyes when the objects of the outward world are brought into powerful relief, with sharp contours and a wealth of admirable colors. The moral world opens its vast perspectives, full of a new, intense brilliancy. The man favored with this happiness— unfortunately so rare and fleeting—feels himself at once more artistic, more just, and more noble, to sum up all in one word. But what is even more unusual in this exceptional state of the mind and the senses which, if compared with the heavy shadows of daily existence might without exaggeration be termed paradisal, is that it cannot be attributed to any very apparent or easily definable cause. Is it the result of abstemious living and a wise diet? This is the first explanation that springs to mind; yet we are obliged to recognize that this marvel, this sort of prodigy, which seems to have been created by some superior, invisible force outside of man, quite frequently appears after he has abused his physical faculties. Shall we say that it is the reward for assiduous prayer and spiritual passion? Certainly, a constant heightening of desire and a spiritual yearning for heaven would be the regimen that is most conducive to creating so intense and glorious a moral health. But by virtue of what absurd law does it sometimes arrive after guilty orgies of the imagination and sophistic abuses of reason, which logically bear the same relation to the honest and reasonable use of the faculties as do the convulsions of a contortionist to healthy gymnastics? This is why I prefer to consider such an abnormal condition of the spirit as a true state of grace, a sort of magic mirror* in which man is invited to see himself as beautiful—that is to say, as he could and should be; a sort of angelic excitation, a call to order in complimentary form. Hence it is that a certain spiritualist school, which has adherents in England and America, considers supernatural phenomena such as ghosts and specters, etc., as the manifestation of a divine will vigilantly endeavoring to awaken in man's mind the memory of invisible realities.

To be sure, this charming and singular state in which all forces are in equilibrium, in which the imagination, however marvelously powerful, does not draw the moral sense toward perilous adventure, in which an exquisite sensitivity is no longer tortured by afflicted nerves, the most common counselors of crime or despair—this marvelous state, I say, appears without harbinger. It arrives as unexpectedly as an apparition. This, too, is a type of haunting, but an intermittent one, from which, if we are wise, we may derive the certainty of a better existence and the hope of attaining it through the daily exercise of our will. This sharp mental activity, this intellectual and sensory enthusiasm, has always appeared to man to be the most perfect of blessings; that is why, thinking only of his immediate pleasure, he has heedlessly violated the laws of his constitution to find in physical sciences, in pharmaceuticals, in the harshest liquors, in the subtlest scents, in all places, and at all times, the means to flee his wretched dwelling, if only for a moment. He seeks, as the author of *Lazare** expresses it, "to carry off Paradise in one go." Alas! the vices of man, however frightful they seem, contain the proof (if only in their infinite applications!) of his taste for the infinite; and yet it is a taste that quite frequently goes astray. One could interpret the common proverb "all roads lead to Rome" in the metaphorical sense and apply it to the moral world; all actions lead to reward or punishment, two forms of eternity. The human spirit brims over with passion; it has enough to spare, to use another trite expression. But this unfortunate spirit possesses a natural depravity, which is as great as its unexpected, quasi-paradoxical aptitude for charity and the most arduous of virtues; and it is also rich in paradox, which allows it to employ that overflow of passion for the furtherance of evil. A man in such a situation never believes he is selling his soul. In his infatuation, he forgets that he is playing with a being subtler than himself, and that if the Spirit of Evil* is allowed to grasp but a single hair, it will lose no time in carrying off the entire head. This evident lord of visible nature (I speak of man) has thus sought to create paradise through pharmacy and fermented beverages, like a madman who would replace solid furniture and real gardens with scenery painted on canvas. It is this corruption of the sense of the infinite, I believe, that is the cause of all of man's guilty excesses, from the solitary, concentrated intoxication of the literary man who, obliged to seek in opium a relief from some physical affliction and having thus discovered a source of morbid pleasures, has gradually made of it his sole comfort, and the sun of his spiritual life, to the most common, vile drunkard who, his brain full of flame and glory, reels ridiculously down littered streets.

Among the drugs most conducive to creating what I call the Artificial Ideal—leaving aside drink, which quickly gives rise to physical furor and drains the spiritual force, and inhalants, the excessive use of which, even while rendering man's imagination more subtle, will gradually sap his physical strength—the two most potent substances, those which are the most accessible and the easiest to use, are hashish and opium. The analysis of the mysterious effects and morbid pleasures these drugs can produce, the punishment that invariably follows their prolonged use, and, finally, the immorality implicated in the pursuit of this false ideal constitute the subject of this study.

The work on opium has already been written, and so brilliantly, from both the medical and poetic viewpoint, that I dare not add anything to it. Therefore, I will content myself with offering the reader, in another study, an analysis of this incomparable book, which has not yet been translated into French in its entirety.* The author, a well-known man of powerful and exquisite sensibilities (today retired and silent), dared to write, with tragic honesty, an account of the pleasures and tortures he once found in opium, and the most dramatic part of this book is that in which he speaks of summoning up the resolution, by superhuman efforts of will, to regain the liberty he had imprudently surrendered.

I shall now speak only of hashish, and shall report the character of its consequences, drawing on numerous testimonials and the detailed written notes of intelligent men who have had long experience with its action. Only I shall cast these documents into a sort of monograph, choosing an individual easy to explain and define as a suitable representative of the type of person most given to experiences of this nature.

II. WHAT IS HASHISH?

The narratives of Marco Polo, like those of our other ancient explorers, have been verified by scholars and should not, therefore, be lightly dismissed. I will not retell his story of how, after having drugged them on the hashish of the old Assassins (or Hashishins), the Old Man of the Mountain confined in a garden of unimaginable delights those of his young disciples to whom he would give a glimpse of paradise—as anticipated reward, so to speak, for their absolute, uncritical obedience.* For full information on the secret society of the Hashishins, I refer the reader to Mr. von Hammer's book* and to Mr. Silvestre de Sacy's article, which appears in volume 16 of the *Mémoires de l'Académie des Inscriptions et Belles-Lettres;* and, on the etymology of the word *assassin*, his letter to the editor of the *Moniteur*, included in issue number 359 of 1809. Herodotus tells us that the Scythians gathered mounds of hemp-seed onto which they cast stones that had been reddened by fire. The joy occasioned by the resulting vapors, which seemed to them more sweetly scented than any that rose from the Greek baths, provoked cries of pure delight.

Hashish, of course, comes to us from the Orient; the stimulating characteristics of hemp were well known in ancient Egypt and its use, under various names, was widespread in India, Algeria, and Arabia Felix. But before our own eyes, we have interesting examples of intoxication brought about by vegetal emanation. Aside from the children who experience unusual bouts of dizziness after playing and rolling in stacks of cut alfalfa, we know that, when hemp is harvested, male and female laborers experience similar effects; they say that the cut plants exude a miasma that maliciously torments their brains. The harvester's head begins to spin and becomes charged with dreams. At times, their limbs grow weak and refuse to serve. We have heard stories of Russian peasants who are occasionally prone to somnambulistic attacks caused, they say, by the hemp-seed oil with which they prepare their food. Who does not know of the extravagances of fowl that have eaten hemp-seed, and the wild enthusiasm of horses that the villagers ready for races, on feast and festival days, with rations of hemp-seed sometimes soaked in wine?

French hemp, however, cannot produce hashish; or at least, after repeated attempts, it has proven unsuitable for this purpose, producing a far less potent drug. Hashish, or Indian hemp, *cannabis indica*, is a plant in the Urticaceae family, and very similar to the hemp grown in our country, except that it does not grow to as great a height. The plant possesses such extraordinary powers of intoxication that it has, for some years, attracted the attention of French scholars and society men. It is more or less valued, depending on its various regional origins; the hashish of Bengal is the most prized by enthusiasts; yet the hashish of Egypt, Constantinople, Persia, and Algeria is pleasing in the same fashion, although to a lesser degree.

Hashish (or herb—that is to say, herb par excellence, as if the Arabs had wished to define in one word the source of all ephemeral pleasure) is known by many names, according to the manner in which it was prepared and the country in which it was gathered: in India, *bhang*; in Africa, *teriaki*; in Algeria and Arabia Felix, *madjound*, etc. The plant must be gathered in season, for only when in bud does it possess full potency; and these budding crowns are the only parts of the plant used in the various preparations about which we shall have something to say.

In the Arab countries, the rich extract of hashish is usually obtained by cooking the plant's freshly culled crowns in butter with a little water. The preparation thus arising, after evaporation has rid it of moisture, resembles a greenish-yellow pomade and retains the unpleasant odor of hashish and rancid butter. In this form, it is taken in small pellets of two to four grams. Because of its repugnant odor, which intensifies over time, the Arabs mix the rich extract into a sweet jam.

The most commonly employed of these preparations is *dawamesk*, a blend of rich extract, sugar, and diverse flavorings, such as vanilla, cinnamon, pistachio, almond, and nutmeg. They even sometimes add cantharides, although for a completely different purpose. In this new form, the taste of the hashish is far from disagreeable, and it can be taken in quantities of fifteen, twenty, and thirty grams, either dissolved in a cup of coffee or wrapped in a bit of bread.

Messrs. Smith, Gastinel, and Decourtive, in their experiments, have endeavored to discover the active principle of hashish. Despite their efforts, its chemical composition remains something of a mystery, but its properties are generally attributed to a resinous material, present in fairly abundant quantities, in the approximate proportion of 10 per 100 parts. The resin is obtained by grinding the dried plant into a coarse powder which, after being washed several times in alcohol, is then distilled and reduced. When it has reached the proper consistency, the remaining substance is treated with water to dissolve the foreign gummy matter, until finally only the pure resin remains.

The paste thus arising is soft, dark green in color and redolent with the characteristic odor of hashish. A quantity of five, ten, or fifteen centigrams is enough to produce staggering effects. But the hashishin, which can be eaten in the form of chocolates or small ginger tablets, gives rise to sensations which, like those of the dawamesk and the rich extract, vary widely in strength and are of an extraordinarily diverse nature. The effects on different constitutions will vary according to the individual's temperament and nervous makeup: at times the hashish will produce an immoderate, irresistible gaiety, at other times a feeling of well-being and contentment, at other times an uneasy sleep traversed with dreams. Certain phenomena, however, are produced quite regularly, especially among those of similar temperament and education; there is a type of unity amid the variety, which will allow me to pass without too much difficulty to the subject I now propose to treat.

In Constantinople, in Algeria, and even in France, a blend of tobacco and hashish is commonly smoked; these phenomena will then appear in a much more moderate and, so to speak, indolent form. I have heard that a recently discovered process of distillation has succeeded in drawing from hashish an essential oil, which appears to contain much more of the active principle than have any of the preparations heretofore known; but I cannot speak of the results with certitude as the subject has not yet been sufficiently studied. Would it not be superfluous to add that coffee, tea, and liquor are powerful adjuvants, which will more or less accelerate the birth of that mysterious intoxication?*

III. THE SERAPHIM THEATER*

What will I feel? What will I see? Astounding marvels and extraordinary spectacles? Is it very beautiful, very terrible, or very dangerous? Those are the questions ordinarily asked, in tones of mingled curiosity and fear, by those who have no experimental knowledge of hashish. One might say that they show a childish impatience to know, like that of people who, having never ventured away from their hearth, find themselves face to face with a stranger who has come from remote, unknown lands. Hashish intoxication is a sort of fantastic landscape to them, a vast theater of conjuring and illusion where all is miraculous and unforeseen. This is a preconception, an unfounded assumption. And since, for the majority of readers and inquisitive souls, the word *hashish* summons images of strangely altered worlds and the promise of prodigious dreams (or rather *hallucinations* which, however, occur less frequently than one might suppose), I will now comment on the most important difference separating the effects of hashish from the phenomena of sleep. In sleep, the adventurous voyage that fills our nights, there is something of the positively miraculous, a miracle whose mystery is dulled by repetitive punctuality. Man's dreams are of two types. The first is filled with his ordinary life, his preoccupations, desires, and vices, which combine in a more or less bizarre manner with objects encountered during the day to randomly fix upon the vast canvas of his memory. This is the natural dream; it is the man himself. But that other type of dream! the absurd and unpredictable dream, which has no bearing on, or connection to, the character, life, and passions of the dreamer! This dream, which I shall term hieroglyphic, evidently represents the supernatural side of life, and it is precisely because of its absurdity that the ancients thought it of divine origin. As this dream cannot be explained by any known cause, they attributed it to a cause external to man; and today, without mentioning oneiromancers, there is still a philosophic school which sees some sort of criticism or counsel in dreams of this nature, a symbolic and moral representation engendered in the very mind of the sleeping man. Such a dream is a dictionary to be studied, a language to which only the wise hold the key.

In hashish intoxication, we find nothing of the kind. Here we never leave the natural dream. Throughout its duration, the intoxication will be nothing but a fantastic dream, thanks to the intensity of colors and the rapidity of the conceptions, but it will always retain the particular quality of the individual. Man wished to dream and now the dream will govern man; but this dream will surely be as the son is to the father. The idler has contrived to artificially introduce an element of the supernatural into his life and thoughts: but he is, after all, and in spite of the heightened intensity of his sensations, only the same man augmented, the same number elevated to a much higher power. He is subjugated, but much to his displeasure, only by himself—that is to say, by the part of himself that is already dominant; *he wished to be an angel and he has become a beast*,* temporarily very powerful, if one might call power an extreme sensitivity that is lacking the will to moderate or exploit it.

Thus let the sophisticates and novices who are curious to taste these exceptional delights take heed; they will find nothing miraculous in hashish, nothing but the excessively natural. The brain and body governed by hashish will yield nothing but their ordinary, individual phenomena, augmented, it is true, in number and energy, but always faithful to their origins. Man will not escape the destiny of his physical and moral temperament: For man's impressions and intimate thoughts, hashish will act as a magnifying mirror, but a pure mirror nonetheless.

Here is the drug we have before us: a morsel of green paste, the size of a nut, the smell of which is so potent that it gives rise to a certain repulsion and bouts of nausea, as will, for that matter, any fine and even appealing scent when carried to its maximum concentration and density, as it were. I might mention in passing that this proposition can be reversed, so that the vilest, most repugnant odor might perhaps become pleasurable were it reduced to its minimum of quantity and expansion. Here, then, is happiness!—it can be contained within an ordinary teaspoon!—happiness with all of its rapture, childishness, and folly! Swallow it without fear; you will not die of it. Your inner organs will suffer no harm. Later, perhaps, a too frequent invocation of the spell will diminish your power of resolve, perhaps you will be less a man than you are today, but the punishment is yet so distant and the future disaster of a nature so difficult to define! Where is the risk? Tomorrow, a slight touch of nervous exhaustion perhaps. Do you not each day risk greater chastisements for less recompense? So the matter is settled: To allow the drug its full range of expansion, you have dissolved your quantity of rich extract in a cup of strong coffee. You have arranged to take it on an empty stomach, postponing your dinner until at least nine or ten o'clock, to allow the poison free reign of action. In an hour a light soup alone will be tolerable. You are now sufficiently bolstered for a long, remarkable voyage. The steam whistle blows, the sails are set, and you, among all the other travelers, are a privileged exception, for you alone are unaware of your destination. You wished it to be so; long live destiny!

I assume that you have taken every precaution to carefully choose the best moment for this adventurous expedition. Every perfect debauch requires perfect leisure. You are aware, more-over, that hashish causes an exaggeration, not only of the individual but also of his circumstances and surroundings; you free yourself of all appointments, all obligations requiring punctuality or precision; you free yourself of thoughts occupied with domestic cares and heartaches. But beware, for cares and anxieties, recollections of obligations demanding your attention at a specific time, will toll like a passing-bell through your intoxicated thoughts, to poison your pleasure. Each care will become a torture and each anxiety a cruel torment. If all of the aforementioned conditions have been met, if the weather is fair and you have found a favorable setting, a variegated landscape or a poetically decorated apartment, and moreover if you might hope for some music, then all is for the better.

There are generally three distinct stages to the drug's action, and it is quite interesting to observe novices experiencing the first symptoms of the first stage. You have heard, of course, the many stories concerning the marvelous effects of hashish; your imagination has fashioned a fixed notion, something resembling an ideal intoxication, and you are burning to discover whether the reality will live up to your expectations. This alone is enough to further distress your already anxious mind, a state so favorable to the poison's invasive, conquering nature. Upon their first experience with the drug, most novitiates complain of its slow action; they await its first signs with puerile impatience and, as the drug does not manifest its presence instantaneously, they utter incredulous cries of protest, much to the amusement of those who know the means by which hashish governs. The first gentle blows, like the warning winds of threatening storms, expand and multiply in the very midst of that incredulity. At first you are seized by an absurd, irresistible mirth. These demonstrations of excessive joy, of which you are almost ashamed, multiply in rapid succession, cutting into the stupor at intervals during which you earnestly struggle to collect yourself. The simplest words, the most trivial ideas, take on new, bizzare appearances; you are even amazed at having previously thought them so simple. Incongruous connections, coincidental resemblances, interminable puns, and comic sketches provide endless delight. The demon has invaded you. This gaiety, as irritating as a tickle, cannot be withstood. From time to time you laugh at yourself, at your foolishness and folly. If your companions are with you, they join in the merriment, laughing at your condition and their own, but, as their laughter is without malice, you take no offense.

This giddy cheer, poignant or languid by turns, this uneasy joy, this insecurity, this permutation of the malady, generally lasts but for a short time. Soon the links that bind your ideas become so frail, the thread that ties your conceptions so tenuous, that only your accomplices understand you. And here again you cannot be completely certain; perhaps they only think they understand you, and the illusion is reciprocal. These outbursts of loud cries and laughter, which resemble explosions, seem like true madness, or at least like the ravings of a madman, to all those who are not similarly intoxicated. Likewise will wisdom, good sense, and the logical thoughts of the sober, prudent observer, delight and amuse you like a particular form of dementia. The roles are reversed. His detachment drives you to extremes of sarcastic mockery. Now is this not really a mysteriously comic situation, when a man is moved to incomprehensible mirth by a person whose condition differs from his own? The lunatic pities the sane man, and henceforth the idea of his own superiority begins to dawn on his intellect's horizon. Soon it will explode like a meteor.

I once witnessed a scene of this sort, pushed to extremes, the grotesque aspect of which was only intelligible to those who knew of, or at least had heard of, the substance and the enormous varieties of effect it can produce even on two supposedly equal intellects. A famous musician, who was unfamiliar with hashish and who, perhaps, knew nothing of it even by name, arrived at a party where almost everyone was under its sway. They tried to give him some idea of its marvelous effects. He smiled graciously, obligingly, upon hearing these fantastic accounts, like a man willing to be *tolerant* for a moment. Those whose wits had been sharpened by the poison quickly sensed his scorn. Their laughter wounded him. The wild demonstrations of mirth and joy, the altered countenances, the strings of puns, the whole dissolute atmosphere of the place irritated him, and pushed him to declare, perhaps more precipitously than he would have wished, *that this extravagance could not be good for an artist and that, moreover, it must be quite exhausting for all involved.* Amusement, like lightning, flashed over their faces. The joy redoubled. "This *extravagance* may be good for you, but it doesn't suit me in the least," said the musician. To this, one of the afflicted egotistically replied, "It suits us, that's all that matters." Our musician did not know whether they were truly mad or merely simulating madness. To his mind, discretion being the better part of valor, he decided to leave. But someone had closed the door and removed the key. Another of the afflicted dropped to one knee before the musician and tearfully begged forgiveness in the name of all the present company; he then insolently declared that in spite of his vast spiritual inferiority which, indeed, moved them to sincere pity, they all felt a deep and abiding affection for him. The musician was persuaded to stay and even, after repeated requests, agreed to play for them. But the sound of the violin spread throughout the room like a new contagion, *gripping* (the word is none too strong) each of the afflicted one by one. They immediately burst into a succession of deep sighs, sudden sobs, a flood of silent tears. The frightened musician approached one man in whom the blissful tempest seemed most tumultuous and asked him if he was suffering very much, and if so, what best might be done to ease the pain. Another member of the group, *a practical man*, suggested soda and bitters. But the afflicted one, his eyes full of ecstasy, gazed at them with indescribable scorn. They wanted to cure a man who suffered from an overabundance of life! A man who was sick with joy!

As this story clearly shows, benevolence plays a great role in the sensations fostered by hashish—a flaccid, indolent, and mute benevolence which is born of enfeebled nerves. Someone once told me of an episode of this sort, which all the more strongly confirms these observations. And since the man in question retained a very precise memory of the sensations he experienced while in that intoxicated state, I could well understand the grotesque and inextricable embarrassment into which he was thrown by that difference in perception of which I spoke a moment ago. I cannot now recall whether this was his first or second experience. Had he taken too strong a dose or had the hashish this time, without any very discernible cause (as is often the case), gathered additional strength and expansion? He told me that amid· the intermingling of pleasure and delight, that supreme delight in which one feels so full of life and so possessed of genius, he had suddenly encountered an object of terror. The beauty of his sensations, which had at first dazzled him, were quickly displaced by horror. He wondered at the fate of both his mind and his body should this state, which he took to be a supernatural one, continually worsen, or should his already strained nerves become ever more delicate. Through the faculty of magnification, which the afflicted's spiritual eye possesses, that fear must have been an ineffable torture. "I was," he said, "like a frightened horse that flies off into a gallop toward the edge of a precipice, wishing to stop, yet knowing that he cannot. Certainly, this was a terrifying gallop. My thoughts, bound to my circumstances and surroundings, to the accidental and to all that the word *chance* implies, had taken an absolute and purely rhapsodic turn. It's too late! I continually repeated to myself in despair. When this mode of feeling—which seemed to me to last an eternity but which in reality had lasted for only several minutes—finally ended, when I thought that I might at last sink into that blissful state so dear to Orientals, which usually follows this tumultuous stage, another wave of *evil fortune* seized me. I was suddenly overwhelmed by a new anxiety, trivial and puerile, for I recalled that I had been invited to a formal soiree. I envisioned myself among this company of intelligent and upright men, each of whom would be in complete control of his faculties. I would be obliged to maintain a calm demeanor, to conceal my agitated mind in the harsh glare of the drawing-room. I was confident that I would succeed, but much shaken when I imagined the efforts of will that such an exertion would cost me. I know not by what chance these words from the Gospel, "Woe to him that causes scandal!" surged into my mind. My misery (misery, alas! only too real) then assumed grandiose proportions. I finally resolved that, despite my great feebleness, I would go to consult a pharmacist, for I knew nothing of reagents and very much wanted to join the gathering with a clear, untroubled mind, as duty demanded. But a sudden thought stopped me at the door to the pharmacy, and I paused there for a moment. As I passed, I had happened to catch a glimpse of myself in the glass of the shop window, and my countenance astonished me. That ashen pallor, those sunken lips, those staring eyes! "I am going to alarm this poor man," I said to myself, "and for what foolishness!" Added to this was the desire to avoid ridicule and the fear of being seen in the shop by someone who would recognize me. This sudden concern for an unknown apothecary dominated my feelings. I believed that this man was as sensitive as I myself was at that hellish instant; and as I also fancied that his ear and his soul, like mine, would tremble at the slightest sound, I decided to enter his shop on tiptoe. I am about to call on this man's charity, I told myself, and I cannot possibly be too discreet. And so I pledged to mute my voice and muffle the sound of my footsteps. Have you ever heard the voice of hashish, that weighty, low, and guttural utterance which may be observed in the longtime eater of opium? The result I obtained was contrary to what I had wished for. Seeking to reassure the pharmacist, I had succeeded only in alarming him. He knew nothing of my illness, and had not even heard tell of it. And yet his gaze reflected considerable curiosity mingled with defiance. Did he take me for an imbecile, a scoundrel, a vagrant? Neither one nor the other, I suppose, but all of these absurd notions crowded my mind. A lengthy explanation (what a chore!) was called for. I had to be explicit on the properties of this drug, as well as its manner of preparation and consumption. I continually repeated that there was no danger for *him*, that I sincerely regretted having disturbed him and that I was simply seeking some means of tempering or mitigating the reaction. Finally—and imagine my consternation upon hearing these words—he requested that I *leave the shop*. This was the reward for all of my charity and excessive concern. I attended my dinner party and caused no scandal. None of the company ever guessed the superhuman efforts I had to exert just to seem like everyone else. But I shall never forget the tortures of this ultrapoetical intoxication, constricted by decorum and thwarted by obligation!"

However naturally inclined I might be to sympathize with all griefs arising from the imagination, I could not help but laugh at this recital. The man who related this tale has not mended his ways. He continues to ask of the accursed green paste the stimulation that he should seek within himself: but, being a prudent, upright, and *worldly* man, he has diminished the doses, which has thus allowed him to commensurately augment their frequency. He later reaped the rotten fruits of this habit.

I now return to the usual progression of the intoxication.

Following this first phase of childish merriment there is something of a momentary calm. But new events are soon heralded by a sensation of chill throughout all the extremities (felt by some people as a severe cold) and a great fatigue distinguishable in the joints and limbs; your fingers turn to butter: and in your head, and throughout your entire being, you feel an embarrassing lethargy and stupefaction. Your eyes grow abnormally large, as if they were being pulled, in every sense, by an implacable ecstasy; your face turns pale. Your lips sink inward and retract, with the sharp intake of breath that we see in men who are consumed by great projects, who are oppressed by weighty thoughts, or who are about to take a plunge. The throat constricts, in a manner of speaking. The palate is parched by a thirst that would be infinitely sweet to satisfy, were not the delights of an indolence, from which it would be misery to stir, far sweeter. Deep, convulsive sighs break from your chest, as if your *former* body could not support the desires and activities of your *new* soul. From time to time an involuntary shudder passes through you, like the sudden starts which, at the end of a long day of labor or during stormy nights, precede final slumber.

Before I continue, I will venture to add one more anecdote, regarding that feeling of chill I mentioned earlier, so as to demonstrate how widely the effects (even those of a purely physical nature) can vary from individual to individual. This time the narrator is a man of letters, and in some passages of his account one can, I believe, find indications of a literary temperament.

"I took a moderate quantity of the rich extract," he told me, "and all was well. The attack of perverse mirth had not lasted long, and by gradations I slipped into a state of languor and amazement bordering on bliss. I was looking forward to long hours of calm and undisturbed delight. Unfortunately, as chance would have it, I was obliged to accompany an acquaintance to the theater. I would bear up with fortitude, I resolved, and disguise the overpowering impulse to succumb to total sedentariness. All of the carriages in my neighborhood were taken, so I steeled myself for a long walk through the streets, surrounded by the discordant din of carriages and the stupid conversation of passers-by, a whole sea of triviality. The slight sensation of coolness that had already begun in my fingertips soon became a penetrating chill, as if I had plunged my hand into a pail of ice water. But far from being unpleasant, this sharp sensation was instead a source of the liveliest enjoyment. And yet it seemed to me that the cold became ever more invasive throughout that interminable walk. Several times I asked the person with me whether he found that the temperature had been dropping steadily; he replied that, on the contrary, the evening was unusually warm. Settled at last in the hall, sitting in my reserved box seat, with three or four hours of relaxation before me, I thought that I had finally reached the promised land. All of the thoughts and feelings that I had been suppressing on the way to the theater, with all of the feeble energy that I could muster, erupted at that moment as I abandoned myself freely to that silent frenzy. An icy chill ran through my body, and yet I saw that people were dressed in light summer clothes, and that some were even wiping their brows with an air of overheated fatigue. An idea suddenly struck me and filled me with delight: I believed that I was a privileged being, that I alone was granted the right to feel a chill in the summer in the hall of a theater. The cold became all at once intolerable, to the point of becoming alarming. But I was above all dominated by the desire to know just how much further the temperature could fall. So complete was this chill, so generalized did it become, that at length I could feel my ideas freeze, in a manner of speaking. I had changed into a thinking pillar of ice; I saw myself as a statue hewn from a single block of ice, and I was proud of this mad hallucination. It excited in me a feeling of moral well-being which I do not know how to define. The certitude that the others in the audience were unaware of my true nature, and my superiority to them, only fed my abominable pleasure; and then, how delightful to think that my companion could not begin to conceive of the bizarre delights that had now taken hold of my spirit! I held the reward for my dissimulation, and these sweet sensations I would keep as my private secret.

"What is more, immediately after entering my box, an abiding darkness descended over my eyes, a darkness which seemed somehow to be allied to the idea of cold. It may well have been that these ideas reinforced each other. You know that hashish always invokes magnificent displays of light, the most glorious splendors, cascades of liquid gold; all lights then are pleasing— those that glimmer in brilliant sheets, those that depend like tinsel from projections and asperities, drawing room candelebra, the dazzle of taper lights, the rose-colored avalanches in the rays of the setting sun. It seemed that the miserable lustre shed here was far too feeble to satisfy this insatiable thirst for light; as I mentioned, I thought that I had entered a world of shadow, which did indeed gradually deepen. I dreamed then of polar nights and eternal winters. As for the stage, it alone was sufficiently lighted, but it was infinitely small and distant, as if seen through the end of an immense stereoscope. I will not tell you that I listened to the actors, for you know how impossible this would be. From time to time I caught a passage or a fragment of a sentence which my mind, like an agile ballerina, employed as a trampoline to spring yet deeper into the land of dreams. You might suppose that, heard in such a manner, a play would be devoid of coherence and logic; let me assure you that this was not the case. I discovered an extremely subtle meaning in the play by way of my distraction. Nothing in it shocked me, and I was a little like that poet who, upon seeing *Esther* performed for the first time, is not surprised when Aman makes his declaration of love to the queen. This is of course the moment when he throws himself at Esther's feet to beg her pardon for his crimes.* If all plays were heard in this manner, they would thereby acquire a great beauty, even those of Racine.

"The actors appeared extremely small and seemed to be drawn with a precision of outline which might be compared to that of Meissonier's painting.* I distinctly saw in great detail, not only the most minute features of their costumes, such as the pattern and cut of the fabric, buttons, etc., but also the line separating the false from the true brow, the white, the blue, and the red, all of the resources of theatrical device. And these lilliputians were bathed in a cold and magical glow, which was similar to the luminous sheen that a sheet of glass imparts to a painting. When I was finally able to leave that cavern of frozen shadows and when, the wild inner visions having subsided, I was brought back to myself, I felt a lassitude more overpowering than any ever caused by long, difficult labor."

At this stage of the intoxication, the drug sharpens the senses and the powers of perception, of taste, sight, smell, hearing—all participate equally in this progression. The eyes pierce the infinite. The ear hears sounds that are almost imperceptible amid even the most tumultuous din. Then the hallucinations begin. By gradations, external objects assume unique appearances in the endless combining and transfiguring of forms. Ideas are distorted; perceptions are confused. Sounds are clothed in colors and colors in music. One might say that this is altogether natural and that every poetic intellect, in its healthy and normal state, could easily conceive of such analogies. But I have already informed the reader that there is nothing really supernatural in the hashish intoxication; only, through the growing faculties of the senses, these analogies assume an unusual purity and force. The mind is penetrated, invaded, and overpowered by their despotic character. Musical notes become numbers, and if you are gifted with any mathematical aptitude, the melody and the harmony, while retaining their sensuous and voluptuous qualities, are transformed into a vast arithmetical operation: numbers engender numbers, the phases and genera- tion of which you follow with inexplicable facility and an agility equal only to that of their execution.

At times you will find that your conscious nature has disap- peared and that objectivity, which is the attribute of pantheistic poets, follows a course of abnormal development. In considering the impressions from outward objects you forget your existence, until you confuse the objects of your senses with the objects of the real world. You stare at a tree that harmoniously rocks in the breeze; in a few seconds what would for a poet be a natural comparison becomes a reality to you. You endow the tree with your passions and desires; its capriciously swaying limbs become your own, so that soon you yourself *are* that tree. Thus, when looking skyward, you behold a bird soaring into the deep azure. At first, the bird seems to *represent* the immortal yearning to soar above earthly concerns. But you have already become that bird. Imagine that you are seated, smoking a pipe. Your attention lingers a moment too long on the spirals of bluish clouds that drift slowly upward from the pipe's bowl. The idea of evapora- tion—slow, uninterrupted, and obsessive—grips your mind and soon you will apply this idea to your own thoughts, to your own thinking process. Through some odd misunderstanding, through a type of transposition or intellectual quip, you feel yourself vanishing into thin air, and you attribute to your pipe (in which you fancy yourself crouched like packed tobacco) the strange ability to *smoke you.*

Fortunately, that interminable fantasy lasts only one minute, as you observe when a lucid interval, which you won with great effort, gives you the chance to glance at the clock. But now you are borne off on a new current of ideas, which will toss you in its living whirlpool for yet another minute, and that minute too will seem an eternity. For the proportions of time and being are thoroughly disrupted by the multiform variety of your feelings and the intensity of your ideas. You could say that many lives are crowded into the compass of one hour. Do you not, then, bear some resemblance to a fantastic novel, which will come to life rather than be written? The equilibrium between the sentient organ and its delights is disturbed; and it is especially from this consideration that springs the blame applicable to this dangerous exercise, in which liberty is surrendered.

When I say hallucination, the word must not be taken in its strictest sense. An extremely important nuance distinguishes pure hallucination, which doctors have had occasion to study, from the hallucination, or rather the disruption of the senses, found in the mental state induced by hashish. In the first case, the hallucination is swift, perfect, and inevitable; moreover, no explanation or cause for it can be found among the world of natural objects. The man whose senses have yielded to the drug will see images and hear sounds that exist only in his imagination. In the second case, the hallucination is progressive, almost voluntary, and it will never be perfect but will ripen through the action of the imagination. And finally, it is grounded in reality. The sound will speak, utter distinct words, but there has, in fact, been a sound. The intoxicated eye will see strange forms; but the same forms and images, before having been clothed in strange or monstrous guise, were simple and natural. The energy and vivacity that is truly expressed in the hashish hallucination does not in the least invalidate this original difference. The one is rooted in the ambient surroundings and present circumstances; the other is not.

That I may better convey to the reader this turbulence of the imagination, this ripening of the dream, this poetic birth to which the mind intoxicated by hashish is subject, I will tell another story. This time, our narrator is not an idle young man, nor even a man of letters, but rather a woman of mature age, curious and possessing an enthusiastic, excitable temperament. Having surrendered to her desire to experience the poison, she described her most powerful visions to a female friend. Here is her account, literally transcribed:

"However new and bizarre were these sensations that arose during the twelve hours of my folly (twelve hours or twenty? truthfully, I do not know), I shall never seek them again. The mental excitation was too sharp, the exhausting aftermath too vast and, I admit, I found something criminal in that childish indulgence. I finally satisfied my curiosity and, moreover, the folly was a communal one, for I was visiting some old friends, where I saw no harm in risking a slight loss of dignity. I would especially tell you that this accursed hashish is a fiendishly perfidious substance; you sometimes think that you have shaken off the intoxication, but the calm is deceptive. Lulls are followed by recurrences. So it was that at about ten o'clock in the evening, I found myself in one of these fleeting calms. I thought that I had been delivered from that superabundance of life which, indeed, had given me so much pleasure, but which, too, was not free of anxiety and fear. I sat down to dinner with great pleasure, having until then prudently refrained from eating. I felt weary, as if I had just returned from a long voyage. But even before I had risen from the table, the delirium seized me again. As a cat springs on a rat, the poison made malicious sport with my poor brain. As you know, I live only a short distance from our friends' château, but even though there was a carriage at my disposal, I was so overwhelmed by the desire to dream, to yield to that irresistible madness, that when they invited me, I gladly agreed to stay for the night in preference to going home. You have seen this château; you know how they have arranged and decorated it; you know that they have provided *all of the modern conveniences* in the sections used by the family and that the other sections, which are usually vacant, have been left untouched, with the former style and decor intact.

They fixed a bedroom for me in this section of the château. They chose the smallest room, a type of boudoir which was somewhat neglected and faded but which nevertheless was not lacking charm. I must describe the room as precisely as I can, so that you might have the clearest possible conception of the marvels and visions to which I fell victim, visions which haunted me throughout the night, without allowing me the leisure to notice the passing of the hours.

"The boudoir* is excessively narrow and confining. Over the upper portion of the ceiling, the cornice rounds into a cupola; narrow and elongated rectangular mirrors occupy most of the walls, separated by panels on which landscapes have been painted in a style as elaborately gaudy as that of the decor. On all four walls, at the height of the cornice, are painted representations of various allegorical figures, some in attitudes of repose, others running or flying about. Above them are brightly colored birds and flowers. Behind the figures and naturally following the curve of the ceiling, which is of fretted gold, rises a trompe l'oeil trelliswork. All of the interstices between the molding and the figures are therefore of gold. Only in the center of the ceiling is the gold interrupted, by the geometric lace of the simulated trellis. Thus, you can see that the room is somewhat like a very sophisticated *cage*, the beautiful cage of an enormous bird. I must add that the night was very lovely, clear, and the moon very bright, to the point that even after I had extinguished the candle, all of the decorations remained visible: not illuminated by my mind's eye, as you might suppose, but by the rays of the moon as it shed a golden lustre over all that embellishment of gold, over the mirrors, and multicolored walls.

"At first I was very astonished to see immense perspectives stretching before me, next to me, on all sides—I saw transparent rivers and verdant landscapes reflected in pools of water as still as glass. You can imagine the effect of the painted panels reflected in the mirrors. Looking upward, I surveyed the ceiling and saw a setting sun as red as molten metal: this was the gold of the ceiling. But I then supposed, because of the trellis, that I was in a sort of cage or a house open to space on all sides. Only the bars of my magnificent prison separated me from the outside. At first I laughed at this illusion, but the longer I gazed directly at it, the more the magic intruded upon my senses, until the visions took on a life of their own, a particular clarity that gave to the scene an aspect of despotic reality. From that moment, my thoughts were dominated by claustrophobia which did not much negate, I must confess, the varied joys I gathered from the spectacle playing out above and around me. I thought that I might remain imprisoned for some time, for thousands of years perhaps, in that splendid cage, in wild landscapes graced by glorious horizons. I dreamed of *Sleeping Beauty*, of atonement and future deliverance. Above my head darted brilliantly colored tropical birds, and as I heard the sound of clinking bells on the bridle of a horse passing on the main road, the impressions of the two senses fused into one identity, and I attributed this mysterious song of brass to the birds, and fancied that they warbled with metal throats.* Their song, evidently, celebrated my captivity.

"Chattering monkeys and mischievous satyrs seemed amused by this prisoner stretched out and condemned to helpless captivity. But all of the mythological divinities gazed at me with charming smiles, as if urging me to be patient and to endure the spell; and the pupils of their eyes slid sideways, as if in an attempt to hold my gaze. From this I concluded that if, because of former evils or past sins forgotten, I was forced to suffer this temporary punishment, then I could, nonetheless, rely on a superior goodness which, even while counseling prudence, would offer more serious pleasures than those of our childhood days. So you see that moral considerations were not absent from my dreams, but I must admit that the pleasure I derived from contemplating these forms and images of brilliant colors, from believing that I was at the center of a fantastic drama, frequently absorbed all of my attention. This state lasted a long while, a very long while... Until morning? This I cannot say. For when I saw the first rays of daylight fill my room, I was quite amazed and, despite mustering every effort to remember, I could not tell whether I had slept or had patiently submitted to a delicious insomnia. A moment ago it was night, and now it was day! And yet hours had passed, so many hours!... the notion, or rather the measurement of time, had been destroyed, and the length of the night could be measured only by the multitude of thoughts that crowded my mind. And long though the night had appeared, from this point of view, it seemed nevertheless to have lasted but a few seconds, or even, perhaps, had taken no material place in eternity.

"I will not tell you of my exhaustion... it was immense. They say that the rapture of poets and artists is similar to what I felt. I had always supposed that the people who are dedicated to aesthetically moving us must themselves be gifted with a re-markably calm temperament. But if the ecstasy I found in a small spoonful of paste at all resembles that which poets and artists feel, then I think that the pleasure the public derives from the poets is purchased at a heavy price, and it was not without a certain contentment, a prosaic satisfaction, that I at last felt *at home* again, in my intellectual *home*, I mean, in real life."

Here, then, is an apparently reasonable woman, but we shall concern ourselves with her narrative only insofar as we may draw from it a few useful notes which will complete this very cursory description of the principal sensations engendered by hashish.

She spoke of sitting down to dinner as a pleasure that had

arrived at an ideal time, at the moment when a temporary lull—which, however, had *seemed* permanent—allowed her to return to herself. Indeed, as I have said, there are deceiving calms and lulls, and hashish often gives rise to extremes of hunger and excessive thirst. The disorienting crisis that this woman complained of, with its enchanting visions lightly touched with dread, failed to bring her a permanent reprieve; rather, the dinner or supper led only to a redoubling of that to which she had resigned herself so patiently, and with such good grace. The tyrannical hunger and the intolerable thirst in question cannot be easily satisfied. For in this exalted state man feels himself to be so far above material things, or is rather so overwhelmed by his intoxication, that he must summon vast reserves of courage merely to lift a bottle or fork.

The final attack brought on by the consumption of a meal is in fact quite violent and something against which it is impossible to struggle. Such a state would soon become insupportable, were it not soon replaced by another stage of intoxication, which, in the aforementioned case, found expression in splendid visions, alternately terrifying and consoling. In this new phase, which the peoples of the East term *kief,* the turbulence and tempests subside, giving way to a calm and immobile beatitude, a glorious resignation. Although you have long since ceased to be your own master, this no longer disturbs you. All notion of time, all painful sensations, have vanished; or if these at times dare to appear, they only do so as transfigured by the dominant sensation, and then, in relation to their usual form, they are what poetic melancholy is to true sorrow.

Before anything else, then, let us note in this woman's narrative (I transcribed it for this purpose), that the hallucination is a sort of bastard, deriving its very being from the external environment; the mind is only a mirror in which the ambient surroundings are reflected and transformed in an exaggerated manner. Next, we shall observe the intervention of that which I shall term the moral hallucination: the subject believes that she is submitting to an expiation; but the feminine temperament, which is so little given to analysis, prevented her from noticing the oddly optimistic character of the aforementioned hallucination. The benevolent gaze of Olympian deities is poeticized by an essentially *hashishin* lustre. I will not say that she suffered remorse, but when her thoughts momentarily turned to melancholy or regret, they were immediately afterward colored by hope. We shall have further occasion to verify this observation.

She spoke of her exhaustion on the following day. This exhaustion, although despotic, is not immediately apparent, so that when it does strike you are caught unawares. For at first, when you are fully aware that a new day is dawning on your life's horizon, you experience a sense of well-being; you feel gifted with a marvelous lightness. But hardly have you risen to your feet when a lingering bout of intoxication chases and grips you, like the remaining trace of the ball and chain to which you recently had been bound. Your enfeebled legs carry you timidly, and you are in constant fear that you might shatter like some fragile object. Your senses at length begin to yield before the influences of a vast languor (there are those who find it not without charm) which spreads over your faculties like mist over a countryside. For several more hours, you are incapable of work as you fall into a sort of lethargy. This, then, is the punishment for the impious prodigality with which you have expended your vital fluids. You have flung your personality to the four winds, and now how difficult it will be to reconcentrate and regather it!

IV. GOD-MADE MAN

But it is time to put aside all of these tricks and great marionettes, brought forth by the smoke of immature minds. Do we not have more serious matters to discuss: the alteration of human feelings and, to sum all up in a word, the *moral* of hashish?

Until this moment, I have written an abridged monograph treating the intoxication; I limited myself to delineating its primary traits—above all, the physical ones. But what is of the greatest importance to the thinking man, I believe, is the knowledge of the poison's action on his intellect—that is to say the magnification, the distortion, and the exaggeration of his usual feelings and moral perceptions, which then, in an extraordinary atmosphere, present a true phenomenon of refraction.

The man who by the strength of his will can deliver himself, after having long been under the dominion of opium or hashish, and despite the weakness engendered by the habit of his servitude, bears a resemblance to an escaped prisoner. He inspires in me more admiration than does the prudent man who, having always carefully avoided temptation, has never transgressed. With respect to opium-eaters, the English frequently employ terms which can only seem excessive to those innocent souls who have never known the terrors of that species of ruin: "enchained," "fettered," "enslaved!" Chains indeed, compared to which all others—chains of duty, chains of illegitimate love— are nothing but gossamer threads and spiderwebs! Appalling marriage of man to himself! "I had become a bounden slave in the trammels of opium, and my labors and my orders had taken a coloring from my dreams," says Ligeia's husband. And we see in many marvelous passages how Edgar Poe, that incomparable poet, that unrefuted philosopher who must always be cited apropos the mysterious maladies of the mind, describes the somber and irresistible attractions of opium!* Egæus the metaphysician, lover of the radiant Berenice, speaks of an alteration to his faculties, an abnormal and monstrous intensity of interest that he is compelled to apply to the contemplation of even the simplest phenomena: "To muse for long unwearied hours with my attention riveted to some frivolous device on the margin, or in the typography of a book; to become absorbed for the better part of a summer's day, in a quaint shadow falling aslant upon the tapestry, or upon the door; to lose myself for an entire night in watching the steady flame of a lamp, or the embers of a fire; to dream away whole days over the perfume of a flower; to repeat monotonously some common word, until the sound, by dint of frequent repetition, ceased to carry any idea whatever to mind; to lose all sense of motion or physical existence, by means of absolute bodily quiescence long and obstinately persevered in;— such were a few of the most common and least pernicious vagaries, induced by a condition of the mental faculties, not, indeed, altogether unparalleled, but certainly bidding defiance to anything like analysis or explanation." And the nervous August Bedloe, who swallows a great quantity of opium before setting forth upon his morning walk, tells us that he derives a curious benefit from this daily poisoning, as the opium endues all things, even the most trivial, with an exaggerated intensity of interest. "In the quivering of a leaf—in the hue of a blade of grass—in the shape of a trefoil—in the humming of a bee—in the gleaming of a dewdrop—in the breathing of the wind—in the faint odors that came from the forest—there came a whole universe of suggestion—a gay and motley train of rhapsodical and immethodical thought."

So he speaks through the mouths of his characters, this master of horror, this prince of mysteries. These two traits of opium are perfectly applicable to hashish. In the first case as in the second, the intellect, formerly at liberty, becomes enslaved, but the word *rhapsodic*, which so aptly defines a train of thought suggested and ordered by the external world and by chance circumstance is, in the case of the hashish intoxication, a more real and terrible truth. Here reason is reduced to a wreckage at the mercy of every current, and the train of thought is *infinitely more* accelerated, infinitely more *rhapsodic.* I believe this demonstrates in a sufficiently clear manner that the immediate effect of hashish is much harsher than that of opium: in a word, much more an enemy of everyday life, much more troubling. I do not know whether ten years of using hashish will lead to disasters equal to those caused by a ten-year regimen of opium. I can say that as far as the present hour and the day after tomorrow are concerned, that the effects of hashish are far more fiendish; one is a peaceful charmer, the other a chaotic demon.

In this final section, I wish to define and analyze the moral ravages brought about by this dangerous and delicious exercise, ravages so great and dangers so profound that those who return from the battle only lightly scathed seem like brave souls who have escaped from the caves of a multiform Proteus, or like an Orpheus who has conquered Hell. You may, if you wish, regard this language as an excessive use of metaphor, but be assured that these stimulant poisons are not only one of the most direct and terrible means employed by the Prince of Darkness to entrap and enslave deplorable humanity, they are also among his most perfect embodiments.

This time, to abridge my task and to clarify my analysis I shall, rather than assembling diverse personal narratives, concentrate a variety of observations into the person of one individual imagined by myself. In his *Confessions,* De Quincey justly asserts that opium, rather than bringing on sleep, on the contrary excites and stimulates the system, but does so only in keeping with a man's own nature. Hence, when judging opium's marvels, it would be absurd to discuss a man who tends cattle, for he would dream only of cattle and pastures; now, I have no desire to describe the dull dreams of a cattleman under the influence of hashish; who would take pleasure in such a recital? Who would even read it? To idealize my subject, I must focus all of its rays within a single circle—I must polarize them; and the tragic circle in which I am going to assemble them will be, as I mentioned, a soul of my choosing, to some extent analogous to what the eighteenth century called the "sensitive man," what the Romantic school now terms the "misunderstood artist," and what families and the bourgeois masses damn with the epithet "original."

A temperament that is half nervous, half bilious is the characteristic most conducive to the development of the intoxication; let us add a cultured mind, versed in the arts of form and color; a tender heart which, though full of pain, is still open to rejuvenation; we shall even, if you will, go so far as to allow certain past transgressions, and if not positive remorse at least regret for time wasted or unwisely spent, as is found among those who have nervous or excessively sensitive temperaments. A taste for metaphysics and a familiarity with the various hypotheses in the philosophy of human destiny would surely not be useless— nor would the love of virtue, of an abstract virtue, stoic or mystical, which is represented, in all of the books on which modern youth feeds, as the highest summit to which the noble soul might aspire. If we add to all of this a morbid acuteness of the senses, which I have omitted as a supererogatory condition, I believe that we have assembled the general elements most commonly found in the sensitive modern man, of the sort we might call "a banal sort of original." Let us now see what will become of that individuality when pushed to undue lengths by hashish. Let us follow this progression of the human imagination to its final, most resplendent way station, to the individual's belief in his own divinity.

If you happen to be one of these souls, you will at the outset find fertile fields with which to gratify your innate love of form and color. In the early stages of your intoxication, colors will be clothed in a new brilliance, and will crowd your brain with triumphant intensity. Whether fine, mediocre, or even dismal, paintings on the ceiling will assume a startling life of their own; the coarsest painted wallpapers covering the worst inn's rooms take on, like splendid dioramas, added dimensions. Nymphs with gleaming skin gaze at you with immense eyes, clearer than sky and water; characters from antiquity, in religious or military uniform, wordlessly confess their most solemn secrets. Sinuosity of line is a very clear language in which you read the anxiety and desire of their souls. Then that mysterious, fleeting state of mind develops, in which the depth of life, troubled by numerous problems, wholly reveals itself in any scene that falls before your eyes, however ordinary or trivial it might be, and in which the first object you encounter becomes a speaking symbol. Fourier and Swedenborg,* the one with his *analogies*, the other with his *correspondences*, are incarnated in the flora and fauna that stretch before you, and rather than instructing you with their voices, they indoctrinate you with form and color. Your comprehension of allegory assumes dimensions you had heretofore never conceived. Let us note in passing that allegory, this highly *spiritual* genre, which inept painters have given us reason to despise but which truly is one of the earliest and most natural forms of poetry, is restored to its legitimate dominance in the mind illumined by this intoxication. Hashish covers this mind with a magic lustre, colors it in solemnity and lights all of its depths. Landscapes of lace, receding horizons, perspectives of cities bleached white by the lurid light of storms, or kindled into flame by the luminous passion of sunsets, depth of space, allegory for the depth of time—dance, the gestures or monologues of an actor, if you happen to be at the theater—the first words you see, if your glance falls upon the printed pages of a book—in short, everything, the very universality of existence rises up before you in unimagined glory. And grammar, even arid grammar, is then endowed with the evocative power of sorcery; words are reborn, clothed in flesh and blood; the noun, in substantive majesty, the adjective, transparent garment which clothes and colors it like a glaze, and the verb, angel of motion, which imparts momentum to the phrase. And music, that other language so cherished by idlers, or by those intellectuals who seek from it a repose amid their varied toil, unfolds the capabilities of your intellect and recites for you the poem of your life; it enters within you, and you mingle with it. Music expresses your passion, not in a vague and obscure manner as it has done previously during informal parties and evenings at the opera, but in a definite, positive manner, each movement of the rhythm delineating a known movement of your soul. Each note becomes a word, and the entire poem that permeates your mind is like a dictionary endowed with life.

To be sure, one must not suppose that these phenomena occur in the mind pell-mell, with the shrill accent of reality and the chaos of the external world. The inner eye transforms all it sees and complements each object, raising it to perfect beauty, so that it might truly be worthy of pleasing. Also developing at this essentially voluptuous and sensual phase is the love of shining waters; through the medium of the intoxication they assume, in the artistic mind, an astonishing importance. Mirrors become a pretext for this reverie, which finds a resemblance to a spiritual thirst and combines with the physical thirst that parches the throat, about which I have previously spoken; harmonious cascades, waterfalls, babbling jets of water, the blue immensity of the sea, all leap, sing, and sleep with an inexpressible charm. Water beckons like a true enchantress, and although I do not much believe in tales of the drug's wild follies, I am not prepared to claim that the contemplation of still pools would be altogether without danger for a soul enamored of space and glass; or that the old fable of the undine would not become a tragic reality for the enthusiast.

I believe that I have sufficiently spoken of the ways in which hashish expands time and space, two ideas that are always linked but which the mind now faces without sadness or fear. The mind gazes with a certain melancholy savor through the depth of the years gone by, audaciously plunges into infinite horizons. It is obvious, I presume, that this abnormal and tyrannical expansion is equally applicable to all feelings and ideas: hence to benevolence, about which I believe I have given a fair enough example; hence to beauty and to love. The idea of beauty must naturally occupy a significant place in the spiritual temperament that I have imagined. Harmony, linear symmetry, eurythmy in movement appear to the dreamer as necessities, as duties not only in relation to all beings in creation but also to himself, and at this stage of the crisis he finds that he is endowed with a marvelous aptitude for understanding the immortal, universal rhythm. And if our fanatic is somewhat lacking in personal beauty, think not that he will long suffer from the truth that confronts him, nor that he will consider himself as a discordant note struck among the harmonious, beautiful worlds of his imagination. The sophistries of hashish are numerous and admirable, generally tending toward optimism, and one of the principal, and most efficient, is that which makes of desire a reality. The same doubtlessly holds true for many situations in ordinary life, but how much more passionately here, and how much more subtly! Indeed, how could this being so adept at understanding harmony, this priest of Beauty, as it were, make an exception, and thus spoil his own theory? Moral beauty and its power, grace and seductions, eloquence and its feats of prowess—all of these ideas soon present themselves as correctives to an indiscreet ugliness, first as consolations, and finally as the perfect disciples serving an imaginary crown.

As for amorous passion, I have heard many men, moved by schoolboy curiosity, question hashish users on this subject. What then must become of the intoxication of love, already so powerful in the natural state, when it is contained within that other intoxication like a sun within a sun? Such is the question raised by the crowd I will call the poseurs of the intellectual world. To reply to the dishonest implication, the part of the question that dares not be spoken, I must refer the inquisitive reader to Pliny,* who has written about the properties of hemp in such a manner as to dispel many illusions on this subject. Furthermore, everyone knows that atony is the expected consequence of the abuse men inflict on their nerves and the substances designed to stimulate them. Now, as we are not concerned here with affective power, but rather with emotion or susceptibility, I will simply ask the reader to consider the ways in which the imagination of a nervous man is pushed to an extraordinary degree by the hashish intoxication becoming as unpredictable as the gale winds of the most forceful hurricane, while his senses are sharpened to a point almost as difficult to define. Thus it will seem that a light touch, even the most innocent of all, a handshake, for example, can have an effect which is multiplied a hundredfold by the heightened state of the soul and the senses and will perhaps very rapidly lead to the syncope that common mortals conceive as the sum of all earthly bliss. But it is certain that hashish reawakens gentle memories in an imagination that often dwells on matters of love, memories to which even pain and sorrow lend a new lustre. It is no less certain that a good portion of sensuality mingles with this mental agitation. Moreover, and this strongly confirms my assertion concerning the immorality of hashish, it would not be uninteresting to point out that a sect of the Shiites (descendants of the old Assassins) carried their worship well beyond the impartial lingam,* that is to say, to the absolute, exclusive worship of the feminine half of the symbol. Hence, since each man is a representation of history, it would be only natural to see an obscene heresy, a monstrous devotion appear in the midst of a mind which has carelessly surrendered its freedom to an infernal drug, a mind which smiles at the utter waste of its own faculties.

Since we have seen, in the materialization of the hashish intoxication, an odd goodwill, extended even to strangers, a sort of philanthropy of pity rather than of love (it is here that we see the first seed of the satanic spirit which will later develop in such an extraordinary manner), but which goes so far as the fear of causing the least pain or mortification to any human being, we can guess the fate of localized sentimentality when applied to a cherished person who plays, or has played, an important part in the moral life of the afflicted person. Religion, worship, prayer, and dreams of happiness flare and explode with the ambitious energy and glow of a fireworks display; like the powder and colored materials of the fire, they dazzle only to perish in the shadows. There is no form of sentimental attachment to which the hashish slave's supple love will not readily lend itself. The desire to offer protection, an ardent and devoted paternalistic feeling, can mingle with a guilty sensuality, which hashish will always be willing to excuse and absolve. It goes further still. If, because of evils past, bitter traces mark the soul of the husband or lover who, in his normal state, finds it altogether impossible to contemplate his somewhat stormy past without sorrow and regret, then these sorrows and regrets will now easily turn to more gentle sensations. The need to pardon renders the imagination more supple and cunning; and in this diabolical drama, which is expressed in the form of lengthy monologues, remorse itself can act as a stimulant, forcefully rekindling the heart's enthusiasm. Yes, remorse! Was I wrong to say that to the truly philosophical mind, hashish seems like the perfect satanic instrument? Remorse, that curious component of pleasure, is soon drowned in the delicious contemplation of remorse, in a sort of voluptuous analysis; and this analysis is so rapid that man, this natural devil (to speak in Swedenborgian terms), fails to see how involuntary it is and how, second by second, he is drawing closer to pure diabolical perfection. He *admires* his remorse and glorifies himself, even as his freedom is slipping from his grasp.

Here then is this fictitious man, this intellectual type of my choosing, who has reached such heights of joy and serenity that he is *compelled* to admire himself. All contradictions are re-solved, all philosophical problems are clear, or so they seem. He finds delight in everything around him. The richness of this new life fills him with inordinate pride. A voice within him (alas! it is his own) tells him: "You are a privileged exception, and you may consider yourself vastly superior to all men; no one could know, nor understand, your thoughts and feelings at this moment; nor could they begin to comprehend the benevolence you feel for them. You are a king who walks unnoticed through the streets, who lives in the solitude of his convictions; but what could it matter to you? Do you not possess that sovereign contempt that renders the soul so gentle?"

And yet we may suppose that at one time or another a caustic memory crosses and corrupts your happiness. A suggestion prompted by the external world may conjure up remembrances of former sorrows, from a past that is painful to contemplate. How many stupid or vile deeds fill the past of this intellectual king, deeds that are truly unworthy of him and his idealized dignity? You may be sure that the man who has taken hashish will courageously confront these critical ghosts, and that he will even know how to derive new elements of pleasure and pride from his disconsolate memories. The evolution of his reasoning may be thus illustrated: The first sensation of pain having passed, he will with curiosity analyze these memories of deeds or feelings that so hindered his own glorification, the causes behind his actions, and the incidental circumstances of his surroundings; and if he fails to find sufficient cause in the circumstances if not to absolve, then at least to diminish his sin, do not imagine he will feel defeated! His reasoning may be observed as easily as the motion of a mechanism behind a glass: "That ridiculous, cowardly, or vile deed, the memory of which so disturbed me for a moment, is completely contrary to my true, prevailing nature, and the very vigor with which I condemn it, the inquisitorial tenacity with which I analyze and judge it, is proof of my exalted, divine capacity for virtue. How many men would be so willing to judge themselves, how many so severe in condemning themselves? And thus he condemns himself, even amid his own self-glorification. Having absorbed the contemplation of ideal virtue, charity, and genius, he voluntarily surrenders to triumphant mental orgies. We have already seen how, playing the role of both penitent and confessor, he sacrilegiously counterfeited the sacrament of penance, thereby easily granting himself absolution. Or worse yet, how in this self-condemnation he found new pastures for his pride. Now, contemplating his virtuous dreams and plans, he convinces himself that he has a natural aptitude for virtue; the ardor with which he embraces this phantom of virtue seems to him sufficient, decisive proof that he possesses the strength and energy necessary to fulfill his ideal. He completely confounds dream and action, and his imagination burns ever brighter before the enchanting display of his own amended, idealized nature, substituting that fascinating image of himself for the real individual, so deficient in resolve, so rich in vanity. And so he ends by proclaiming his apotheosis in these clear and simple terms, which for him represent a whole world of abominable pleasures: "*I am the most virtuous of all men!*"

Does this not remind you of Jean-Jacques,* who, after having confessed to the world, not without a certain pleasure, also dared to utter the same triumphant cry (or at least the difference is slight), with the same sincerity and conviction? The enthusiasm with which he admired virtue and the excess of nervous sensitivity which brought a tear to his eye at the sight of a worthy action or at the mere meditation on all of the worthy actions he would have liked to perform, endowed him with an exaggerated idea of his own moral worth. Jean-Jacques became intoxicated without using hashish.

Shall I pursue the analysis of this all-conquering monomania? Shall I report how, while in the thrall of the poison, our man soon places himself at the center of the universe? How he becomes the extreme incarnation of the proverb which says that "passion reigns sovereign over all"? He believes in his own virtue and genius—can we not anticipate the outcome? All outward objects are so many suggestions which stimulate worlds of thought, all of them more intensely colored, more glorious, and more subtle, and all clothed in a magical gloss. "The superb cities," he tells himself, its buildings lined up in rows like stage sets—the shining sails of the boats as they balance upon the rippling waters of the harbor in a scene of nostalgic nonchalance seem to translate his own thought: "When do we set sail for happiness?"—these museums crowded with beautiful forms and startling colors—these libraries that hold the works of Science and the dreams of the Muse—these musical instruments that sing in unison—these female enchant-resses, rendered still more charming by the science of their adornment and the economy of gaze—all of these marvels have been made *for me, for me, for me*! Humanity has labored, has been martyred and immolated, for me!—to serve as fodder, as *pabulum*, for my insatiable appetite for emotion, knowledge, and beauty!" I will skip ahead and summarize. No one will be astonished that a final, crowning thought springs from the dreamer's brain: *I have become God!* that a savage, ardent cry explodes from his chest with such energy and force that if an intoxicated man could make his wish his power, and his thought a deed, that cry would topple the angels lining the paths of heaven: "I am a God!" But soon this pride subsides, the tempest settles into a relaxed calm, and he sees the universality of all creatures colored by a sulfurous dawn. If by chance some vague memory slips into the ecstatic soul of this pathetic man—"Is there not another God?"—you may be sure that he would walk in *his* presence with head held high and, before *him*, fearlessly discuss his projects.

Which French philosopher is it who said, in mockery of modern German doctrines, "I am a god who has not dined well"? That irony would fail to make an impression on a man under the sway of hashish; he would calmly reply: "I may not have dined well, yet I am a God!"

V. MORAL

But alas, the morrow! the terrible morrow! when the feebleness of your body, the nerves worn thin to the point of breaking, the irritating urge to cry, the weak state of both mind and body—to the point that you are incapable of attending to any duty—tell you that you have played a forbidden game. Hideous nature, stripped of the previous day's glowing raiment, resembles the dreary relics of last night's festival. Your will, the most precious of all faculties, is subject to the most serious attack. It is said, and this is almost true, that this substance does no physical harm, or at least no serious physical harm. But to what extent can we claim that a man who is incapable of action, who can do nothing but dream, is truly healthy, even if all his bodily constitution flourishes? Now, we are familiar enough with human nature to know that a man who can instantaneously obtain all of the ecstasies of heaven and earth by swallowing a small spoonful of paste will never earn the thousandth part of them through his own labor. Can you imagine a State whose citizens all took hashish? What citizens! What soldiers! What legislators! Even in the East, where the use of hashish is so widespread, some governments have understood the need to put the drug under ban. Assuredly, it is forbidden to man, lest he suffer a fall from grace or intellectual death, to disorder the primordial conditions of his existence and to disrupt the equilibrium between his faculties and the conditions in which they were intended to operate; in a word, to tamper with his destiny, substituting for it a new kind of destiny. Let us remember Melmoth, that admirable symbol.* His horrible suffering lies in the discrepancy between his marvelous powers, instantaneously acquired through a satanic pact, and the surroundings in which, as God's creature, he is condemned to live. And not one of those whom he tries to convince will agree to purchase from him, under the same conditions, this terrible privilege. To be sure, any man who does not accept life's conditions is selling his soul. It is easy to grasp the connection between the satanic creations of poets and the creatures who have yielded to the influence of the stimulant drugs. Man wished to be God, and soon he has, by virtue of an ungovernable moral law, fallen lower than the level of his true nature. He has sold his soul to the lowest bidder.

Balzac evidently thought that the man who was made to surrender his self-command could know no greater shame or suffering. One night I saw him at a party at which the prodigious effects of hashish were being discussed.* He listened and asked questions with amusing attentiveness and enthusiasm. The people who knew him concluded that he must be genuinely interested. But the idea that a man could lose control of his intellectual processes apparently came as a great shock to him. Someone offered him the dawamesk; he examined it, sniffed it, and handed it back without having tried it. His expressive face dramatically betrayed the battle between his almost childlike curiosity and his loathing of self-abdication. His love of dignity prevailed. Indeed, it is quite impossible to conceive by what means this theoretician of the human will, this spiritual twin of Louis Lambert, should voluntarily surrender a particle of that precious *substance.**

In spite of the admirable services rendered by ether and chloroform, it seems to me that from the point of view of spiritualist philosophy, the same moral stigma attaches to all modern inventions which tend to limit human freedom and indispensable pain.* It was not without a certain admiration that I once listened to an army officer's paradoxical story. A French general had undergone a cruel operation at El-Aghouat, and died during it, despite the use of chloroform. This general was a very brave man and, what is more, someone to whom the term *chivalrous* naturally applied. "It wasn't the chloroform that was needed," the officer told me, "but the presence of his troops and the delightful sounds of the military band. With that, he might have been saved!" The surgeon was not of the same opinion, but the chaplain would certainly have applauded those sentiments.

Now, after all of these considerations, it would be truly superfluous to dwell on the immorality of hashish. If I compare it to a suicide, to a slow suicide, or a murderous weapon that is always sharp and bloody, no reasonable soul would disagree. If I liken it to sorcery and magic which, by the art whose subtle power and occult methods (methods whose very efficacity prove them false) would conquer regions forbidden to man, or permitted to only those who are deemed worthy of them, no philosophical soul would object. If the Church condemns sorcery and magic, it is because they are contrary to the intentions of God, because they abolish the accomplishments of time, and would render the conditions of purity and morality superfluous—and because the Church will accept as legitimate and true only those riches earned by assiduous good intention. The gambler who has found a sure means of winning is called a swindler; what then should we call the man who wishes to purchase happiness and genius for the price of a few coins? In the very infallibility of the means lies its immorality, just as the supposed infallibility of magic lies in the diabolical stigma with which it is attached.

Need I add that hashish, like all solitary pleasures, renders the individual useless to his fellow man, that it and society superfluous to the individual, continually leads him to admire himself and precipitates him day by day toward the very brink of the luminous abyss in which he admires his Narcissan face?

And further, what if, at the price of his dignity, his honesty, and his free reasoning, man could derive great mental benefits from hashish, using it to transform himself into a sort of thinking machine, a fecund instrument? I have often heard this question asked, and I will provide an answer. First, as I have explained at some length, hashish reveals nothing to the individual but the individual himself. It is true that this individual is, so to speak, at least trebled in effect and pushed to his limits, and, as it is equally certain that the remembrances of his impressions will survive the orgy, the hopes of the *utilitarians* appear to be, at first glance, not wholly devoid of reason. But I would ask them to notice that these thoughts, by which they set such great store, are not really as beautiful as they appear beneath their temporary disguises and magical tinsel trappings. Such thoughts belong to the earth rather than to heaven and owe a great part of their beauty to nervous irritation, to the eagerness with which the mind embraces them. And then, this hope is but a vicious circle: let us admit for a moment that hashish creates, or at least increases, genius; people fail to remember that hashish, by its very nature, disturbs the intellectual system, and thus it gives with one hand what it takes away with the other—that is to say, it feeds the imagination, without allowing one to profit by the gain. Finally, even supposing a man were adroit and strong enough to elude this alternative, we must consider another inevitable and terrible danger, which is true of all habits: they all rapidly become dependencies. He who would resort to a poison in order to think would soon be incapable of thinking *without* the poison. Can you imagine this awful sort of man whose paralyzed imagination can no longer function without the benefit of hashish or opium?

In philosophical studies we see that the human mind, imitating the course of stars, follows a curve that inevitably leads it back to its point of departure. To conclude is to close a circle. Earlier I mentioned that marvelous state into which the mind of man is at times thrown as if by a special grace. I have said that man has always yearned for the infinite, has always been driven by a desire to revive his hopes, has demonstrated in all countries and at all times a frantic appetite for all substances, however dangerous, which, in exalting his personality, might for an instant reveal to his astonished eyes this one-time paradise, the object of all worldly desire; and, finally, this hazardous impulse, in pushing him unconsciously toward the very brink of hell, has thus testified to his original grandeur. But man is not so abandoned, so bereft of honest ways of reaching heaven, that he should have to invoke sorcery and pharmacy; he need not sell his soul to pay for the affection and the luxurious caresses of the houris. What is a paradise purchased at the cost of eternal salvation? I imagine a man (should I say a Brahman, a poet, or a Christian philosopher?) stationed high on top of a spiritual Olympus; surrounding him are the Muses of Raphael or Mantegna,* who, to give him solace during his arduous fast and untiring prayers, devise their noblest dances and gaze at him with shining eyes, showing their most brilliant smiles; divine Apollo, master of all knowledge (he of Francheville,* Albrecht Dürer, Goltzius,* or anyone else—what does it matter? Is there not but one Apollo, for all those who are worthy of him?) lovingly caresses from his bow its most vibrant melodies. The multitude below, at the foot of the mountain, in the brambles and in the mud, the human flock, the troop of islanders, feign grins of joy and utter a succession of tremendous yells, drawn forth by the poison's sting; and the disconsolate poet says to himself: "These poor souls who have neither fasted nor prayed, who have rejected redemption through honorable toil, ask the black arts to all at once raise them up to the realm of a supernatural existence. Magic dupes them and kindles a false joy, a false light, while we, the poets and philosophers, have redeemed our soul through daily work and meditation; through the assiduous exercise of our will and our solid nobility of purpose, we have created a garden of true beauty for our enjoyment. Having trusted in the expression which says that *faith moves mountains*, we can enjoy the miracle that God alone grants us!"

An Opium-Eater

I. RHETORICAL PRECAUTIONS

"Oh! just, subtle, and mighty opium! that to the hearts of poor and rich alike, for the wounds that will never heal, and for the pangs that tempt the spirit to rebel, bringest an assuaging balm; eloquent opium! that with thy potent rhetoric stealest away the purposes of wrath; to the guilty man for one night gives back the hopes of his youth, and hands washed pure from blood; and to the proud man, a brief oblivion for

wrongs undressed and insults unaveng'd;

that summonest to the chancery of dreams, for the triumphs of suffering innocence, false witness; and confoundest perjury; and dost reverse the sentences of unrighteous judges. Thou buildest upon the bosom of darkness, out of the fantastic imagery of the brain, cities and temples beyond the art of Phidias and Praxiteles—beyond the splendor of Babylon and Hecatompylos; and from the anarchy of dreaming sleep callest into sunny light the faces of long-buried beauties and the blessed household countenances, cleansed from the dishonors of the grave. Thou only givest these gifts to man; and thou hast the keys of paradise, oh, just, subtle, and mighty opium!"* But before the author found the audacity to utter this cry, as violent as the recognition of love, in honor of his cherished opium, what ruses, what rhetorical precautions! First are the eternal allegations of those who have made a compromising confession and have, for all that, almost decided to enjoy them:

"I here present the record of a remarkable period in my life; I trust that it will prove not merely an interesting record but in a considerable degree, useful and instructive. In *that* hope it is that

I have drawn it up; and *that* must be my apology for breaking through that delicate and honorable reserve which, for the most part, restrains us from the public exposure of our own errors and infirmities. Nothing, indeed, is more revolting to English feelings than the spectacle of a human being obtruding on our notice his moral ulcers or scars and tearing away that decent drapery which time, or indulgence to human frailty, may have drawn over them."

He adds, moreover, that guilt and misery generally shrink from public notice and even in the grave will sometimes sequester themselves from the general population of the cemetery, as if declining to claim fellowship with the great family of man. But in the case of the Opium-Eater, it is a question not so much of guilt as of weakness (and, furthermore, a weakness so easy to excuse!) as he will prove in a preliminary biography; thereafter, the benefit resulting to others from the record of an experience purchased at so heavy a price might compensate for any violence done to moral modesty, and justify a breach of the general rule.

In this notice to the reader, we find some information concerning that mysterious people, the opium-eaters, that meditative nation lost within the heart of the busy nation. They are numerous—more so than one might believe. Among them are professors and philosophers, a lord of high office, an under-secretary of state. If one class of society, comparatively so limited, could furnish so many cases, and *that* within the knowledge of a single individual, what frightening numbers would not the entire population of England furnish! Three pharmacists, in widely remote quarters of London, affirmed that the number of *amateur* opium-eaters was (in 1821) immense and that the difficulty of distinguishing these persons, to whom habit had rendered opium a sort of necessity, from such as were purchasing it with a view to reprehensible ends,* occasioned them daily problems. But opium infiltrates all reaches of society, and in Manchester, on a Saturday afternoon, the counters of the druggists are strewn with pills, in preparation for the evening's anticipated demand. For the factory laborers, opium is an affordable pleasure, for the lowness of wages would not allow them to indulge in the costly orgy of ale and spirits. But you may take it for granted that, wages rising, the English workers would not abandon opium to return to the coarse enjoyments of alcohol. The seeds of the fascination are sown; the will is subdued; the memory of the pleasure exercises its eternal tyranny.

If opium can so thoroughly console those natures that have been trampled and defeated by harsh and thankless daily toil, what then must be its effect upon a subtle and educated intellect, upon a passionate and cultured imagination, especially one which has, from an early age, been replenished and nourished on sorrow—upon an intellect marked by endless musings, an intellect "touched with pensiveness,"* to employ our author's astonishing expression? Such is the subject of the marvelous book which I shall unfurl like a fantastic tapestry before the reader's eyes. I will, I shall venture to say, summarize extensively, for De Quincey is essentially a digressive writer; *humorist* is the term that most aptly fits him. In one passage, he compares his thought to a caduceus,* a simple baton that derives its essense and all of its charm from the complicted foliage and flowers in which it is twined. So that the reader should lose nothing of the moving scenes which compose the substance of his book, and, because the space at my disposal is restricted, I shall be obliged, to my great regret, to omit many highy amusing morsels, many exquisite essays that do not directly deal with opium but simply serve to *illustrate* the character of the opium-eater. And yet the work is still quite forceful even in this condensed form, even as a simple extract.

The work (*Confessions of an English Opium-Eater, Being an*

Extract from the Life of a Scholar) is divided into two sections: the first is the *Confessions;* the second, their sequel, is the *Suspiria de Profundis.* Each section is divided into various subsections, some of which I will omit because they serve as corollaries or appendices. The divisions of the first section are perfectly simple and logical, arising from the subject itself: "Preliminary Confessions," "The Pleasures of Opium," "The Tortures of Opium." The purpose of the "Preliminary Confessions," upon which I shall dwell at some length, is easy to see. The author, who has sought to elicit strong interest in a subject as apparently monotonous as the description of an intoxication, goes to great lengths to demonstrate to just what extent he is blameless; he attempts to elicit a feeling of sympathy for his own person, from which the whole work will benefit. Finally, and this is of immense importance, certain accidents—perhaps common enough in themselves but particularly important and serious because of the sensitivity of the person who experienced them— become the key, so to speak, to the extraordinary visions and sensations that will later return to torment his mind. Many an old man, leaning his elbows on a tavern table, sees himself surrounded by his former companions; his drunkenness springs out of his vanished youth. In a like manner, the events narrated in the *Confessions* will occupy an important part of the later visions. They will come back to life like those dreams that are nothing but memories, distorted or transformed by the obsessions of a difficult day.

II. PRELIMINARY CONFESSIONS

No, it was not as a source of idle, guilty pleasure that he first began the use of opium, but simply as a relief from severe stomach pains, the result of cruel days of famine that dated from his earliest youth; and it was in his twenty-eighth year that he first made the acquaintance of the affliction and its remedy, following an epoch of relative happiness, security, and well-being. We shall soon see the circumstances that gave rise to these fateful pangs of anguish.

The future *opium-eater* was seven years old when his father died, leaving him to the care of guardians, who had him sent away to various schools for the first stage of his education.* He was very soon distinguished for his literary attainments, especially for an early knowledge of Greek. At thirteen, he wrote Greek; at fifteen, he not only composed Greek verses in lyric meters but could converse in Greek fluently and without embarrassment, an ability which he owed to the habit of daily improvising into Greek a translation of the English newspapers. Ransacking his memory and imagination for a crowd of periphrastic phrases, to express absolutely modern ideas and images in a dead language, was an exercise that gave him a compass of diction of far greater depth and breadth than that which would have been developed by dull translations of purely literary essays. "That boy," said one of his masters, pointing him out to a stranger, "could harangue an Athenian mob better than you or I could address an English one." Unfortunately, our precocious Hellenist was taken away from this excellent master; and, after having been transferred to the care, first of a miserable pedagogue, who was in a perpetual panic lest the child should expose his ignorance, and finally to that of a worthy and respectable professor. But he, too, sinned through ommission, and his lack of elegance and the meagerness of his understanding were a far cry from the ardent and brilliant erudition of his favorite master. It is a bad thing for a boy to be, and to know himself, far beyond his tutors. They translated Sophocles and, before the lesson began, the zealous professor, the *archididascalus,** prepared with lexicon and grammar for any difficulties he might find in the choruses, thus purging his lessons in advance of any hesitation and difficulty. Meantime, the young man (he was approaching his seventeenth birthday) was burning to go to University. Unfortunately, his earnest attempts to persuade his guardians on this subject were all to no avail. One, a man who was worthy and reasonable, lived at a distance; two of the other three resigned their authority into the hands of the fourth; and this fourth is depicted as the most haughty, obstinate man in the world, and the most in love with the exercise of his own will. Our adventurous young man seized the initiative; he ran away from school. He wrote to a most charming and excellent woman, undoubtedly a family friend who had once held the child on her knee, requesting that she lend him five guineas. A kind, maternal response soon arrived, with double of what he had asked. He had remaining from his pocket money two guineas, and twelve guineas seemed an infinite fortune to a child who had yet known nothing of life's daily necessities. He had only to execute his plan. The following passage is one which I could not bring myself to abridge. Indeed, the reader should be given the opportunity to experience firsthand, from time to time, the author's penetrating, *feminine* style.*

"It is a just remark of Dr. Johnson's (and what cannot often be said of his remarks, it is a very feeling one), that we never do anything consciously for the last time, (of things, that is, which we have long been in the habit of doing) without a sadness of heart. This truth I felt deeply when I came to leave a place which I did not love, and where I had not been happy. On the evening before I left forever, I was saddened when the ancient and lofty classroom resounded with the evening service, per-formed for the last time in my hearing; and at night, when the roll of names was called and mine, as usual, was called first, I stepped forward, and, passing the headmaster who was standing by, I bowed to him, and I looked earnestly in his face, thinking to myself: 'He is old and infirm, and I shall not see him again in this world!' I was right; I never *did* see him again. He looked at me complacently, smiled good-naturedly, returned my salutation or rather, my valediction, and we parted, though he knew it not, forever. I could not reverence him intellectually; but he had always been kind to me, and had allowed me many indulgences, and I grieved at the thought of the mortification I should inflict on him.

"The morning came which was to launch me into the world, and from which my whole succeeding life has, in many important points, taken its coloring. I lodged in the headmaster's house, and had been allowed, from my first entrance, the indulgence of a private room, which I used both as a bedroom and as a study. At half after three I rose, and gazed with deep emotion at the ancient towers of _____,* dressed in earliest light, and beginning to crimson with the radiant luster of a cloudless June morning. I was firm and immovable in my purpose; but yet agitated by anticipation of uncertain danger and misfortune; and, if I could have foreseen the tempest and perfect hailstorm of affliction which soon fell upon me, well might I have been agitated. To this agitation the deep peace of the morning presented an affecting contrast, and in some degree a medicine. The silence was more profound than that of midnight; and to me the silence of a summer morning is more touching than all other silence, because, the light being broad and strong, as that of noonday during other seasons of the year, it seems to differ from perfect day, chiefly because man is not yet abroad; and thus, the peace of nature, and of the innocent creatures of God, seems to be secure and deep, only so long as the presence of man, and his restless and unquiet spirit, are not there to trouble its sanctity. I dressed, took my hat and gloves, and lingered for a moment in the room. For the last year and a half, this room had been my pensive citadel; here I had read and studied through all hours of night; and, though it was true that for the latter part of this time

I, who was framed for love and gentle affections, had lost my joy and happiness, during the strife and fever of contention with my guardian; yet, on the other hand, as a boy so passionately fond of books, and dedicated to intellectual pursuits, I could not fail to have enjoyed many happy hours in the midst of general dejection. I wept as I looked around, at the chair, hearth, writing table, and other familiar objects, knowing that I looked upon them for the last time. Whilst I write this, it is eighteen years ago; and yet, at this moment, I see distinctly, as if it were yesterday, the contours and expression of the object on which I fixed my parting gaze. It was a portrait of the lovely ____,† which hung over the mantelpiece; the eyes and mouth of which were so beautiful, and the whole countenance so radiant with serenity and divine tranquillity, that I had a thousand times laid down my pen or my book to gather consolation from it, as a devotee from his patron saint. Whilst I was yet gazing upon it, the deep tones of the clock proclaimed that it was four o'clock. I went up to the picture, kissed it, and gently walked out, closing the door forever!

"So blended and intertwisted in this life are occasions of laughter and tears, that I cannot yet recall without smiling, an incident which occurred at that time, and which had nearly put a stop to the immediate execution of my plan. I had a trunk of enormous weight; for, besides my clothes, it contained nearly all my library. The difficulty was to have this transported to a carrier's; my room was at an aerial elevation, and (what was worse) the staircase, which communicated with this angle of the building, was accessible only by a gallery, which passed the headmaster's bedroom door. I was a favorite with all the servants; and knowing that any of them would act confidentially, I communicated my embarrassment to one of the headmaster's

---

†The lady of the ten guineas, perhaps.*

grooms. The groom swore he would do anything I wished; and when the time arrived, went upstairs to bring down the trunk. This I much feared was beyond the strength of any one man; however, the groom was a man

> *With Atlantean shoulders, fit to bear*
> *The weight of mightiest monarchies;**

and had a back as spacious as the Salisbury Plain. He insisted on bringing down the trunk alone, whilst I stood waiting at the foot of the last flight of stairs in anxiety for the event. For some time I heard him descending with slow and firm steps; but unfortunately, from his trepidation, as he drew near the dangerous quarter, within a few steps of the gallery, his foot slipped; and the mighty burden, falling from his shoulders, gained such momentum at each step of the descent that, on reaching the bottom, it trundled, or rather leaped, right across, with the uproar of twenty devils, against the very bedroom door of the *archididascalus*. My first thought was that all was lost, and that my only chance for executing a retreat was to sacrifice my baggage. However, on reflection, I determined to abide the issue. The groom was in a frightful panic, both on his account and on mine; but in spite of this, so irresistibly had the sense of the ludicrous, in this unhappy *contretemps*, taken possession of his fancy, that he sang out a long, loud, and canorous peal of laughter, that might have wakened the *Seven Sleepers*. At the sound of this resonant merriment, within the very ears of insulted authority, I could not myself forbear joining in it; subdued, not so much by the unhappy *étourderie* of the trunk, as by the disquieting effect it had upon the groom. We both expected, as a matter of course, that the doctor would sally out of his room, for, in general, if but a mouse stirred, he sprang out like a mastiff from the kennel. Strange to say, however, on this occasion, when the noise of laughter had ceased, no sound, or rustling even, was to be heard in the bedroom. The doctor had a painful complaint which, sometimes keeping him awake, made his sleep, perhaps, when it *did* arrive, the deeper. Gathering courage from the silence, the groom hoisted his burden again, and accomplished the remainder of his descent without accident. I waited until I saw the trunk placed on a wheelbarrow and on its road to the carrier's; then, with Providence my guide,* I set off on foot—carrying a small parcel, with some articles of dress under my arm, a favorite English poet* in one pocket, and a small 12mo. volume, containing about nine plays of Euripides, in the other."

Our student had originally intended to proceed to Westmoreland; but an accident,* which he does not explain to us, gave a different direction to his wanderings and he then bent his steps toward North Wales. After roaming about for some time in Denbighshire, Merionethshire, and Caernarvonshire, he took lodgings in a small neat house in B———.* But an incident which crossed his young pride in a most amusing manner soon drove him out to wander again. His landlady had been a lady's maid, or a nurse, in the family of a bishop. The proudest class of people in England (or, at any rate, the class whose pride is most apparent) are the families of bishops. In a little town like B———, merely to have lived in the bishop's family conferred some distinction, so that what "mylord" said, what "mylord" did, how useful he was in Parliament, and how indispensable at Oxford, formed the daily burden of her talk. Perhaps in her eyes, the young man appeared inadequately impressed with the bishop's importance. One day, she had been to pay her respects to the bishop and his family; she had given him, in response to his questions, an account of her household economy. Learning that she let her apartments, the worthy bishop had taken occasion to caution her as to her selection of tenants. "For," said he, "you must recollect, Betty, that this place is on the main road to the Head;* so that multitudes of Irish swindlers, running away from their debts into

England—and of English swindlers running away from their debts to the Isle of Man—are likely to take this place in their route." And the good lady proudly reported her conversation to the young man, not forgetting to add her reply to the bishop: "Oh! mylord, I really don't think this young gentleman is a swindler, because..." —"You don't think I'm a swindler!" replied the exasperated young student, "for the future I shall spare you the trouble of thinking about such things." And he prepared for his departure. The good woman seemed disposed to make some concessions, but as the young man had spoken words of indignation directed at the bishop himself, reconciliation then became impossible. "I was," he said, "truly irritated at the bishop's having suggested any grounds of suspicion against a person whom he had never even seen; and I thought of letting him know my mind in Greek; which, at the same time that it would furnish some presumption that I was no swindler, would also (I hoped) compel him to reply in the same language; in which case, I doubted not to make it appear, that if I was not so rich as his lordship, I was a far better Grecian. Calmer thoughts drove this boyish project from my mind.. "

So he resumed his life of wandering, but as he lived from inn to inn, his money was very rapidly spent. In a fortnight, he was reduced to one meal a day. Exercise and mountain air acted vigorously on his youthful stomach, and soon he began to suffer greatly on this slender regimen, for his single meal consisted solely of coffee or tea. Even this, however, soon became an impossible luxury and, so long as he remained in Wales, he subsisted entirely on blackberries, hips, and haws. Casual hospitalities he now and then received, in return for such small writing services as he could render. Sometimes he wrote letters of business for cottagers who happened to have relatives in Liverpool or London. More often, they were love letters, which the young women who had lived as servants in Shrewsbury, or other towns on the English border, had asked him to write to the sweethearts they had left behind. He relates a touching episode of this nature. In a sequestered part of Merionethshire, near the village of Llan-y-styndw,* he was entertained for upwards of three days by a family of young people with an affectionate and cordial hospitality. The family consisted of four sisters and three brothers, all of whom spoke English, and all remarkable for their elegance and native beauty. He wrote a letter about prize money for one of the brothers, who had served on board a battleship and, more privately, two love letters for two of the sisters. These girls, by their simplicity, candor, and natural and blushing modesty, evoked the transparent and delicate charm of keep-sakes.* In the midst of their confusion and blushes as they dictated their instructions, he discovered that what they wished was that their letters should be of the kind as was consistent with maidenly pride; and they were as much pleased with the way in which he had expressed their thoughts as they were astonished at his having so readily discovered them. But one morning he was met with a singular setback, which set in motion the latter stage of his sufferings; one of the brothers explained to him that their parents had gone to an annual meeting of Methodists, held at Caernarvon, and were expected to return that day. These old people, with their harsh demeanor, answered "*Dym Sassenach*" (*no English*) to all of the young man's addresses. "For, though they spoke warmly to their parents on my behalf, I easily understood that my talent for writing love letters would do as little to recommend me, with two grave Welsh Methodists, as my Greek Sapphics or Alcaics." And fearing that the gracious hospitality of his young friends would become cruel charity when connected with these grumbling sexagenarians, he resumed his unusual pilgrimage.

The author fails to tell us by what ingenious means he managed, despite his poverty, to get to London.* But here this poverty, as bitter as it had been, became positively fierce, almost a daily agony. Just imagine sixteen weeks of suffering caused by almost constant hunger, which was barely appeased by a few morsels of bread subtly removed from the table of a man about whom we shall soon speak; two months of sleeping in the open air; and finally the intermittent anguished sleep that came to disquiet his already troubled mind. His schoolboy adventure certainly cost him dear. When the inclement weather came on, as if to augment sufferings which already seemed as if they could get no worse, he discovered, by good fortune, a house in which he could take shelter, but what shelter! The same person whose breakfast he shared (the man thought he was ill and was ignorant of the full extent of his deprivation) allowed him to sleep in the large unoccupied house which he tenanted. Unoccupied it was, for there was no household in it, nor any furniture save for a table and a few chairs; a dusty desert, full of rats. In the midst of this desolation, however, lived a poor little girl, about ten years of age, but she seemed hunger-bitten* and sufferings of that sort make children look older than their years. Whether she was the illegitimate daughter of the man in question or only a servant, the author could not ascertain. The poor abandoned girl expressed great joy when she found that she was to henceforth have a companion through the dark hours of the night. The house was vast; and from the want of furniture, the scampering of the rats echoed prodigiously through the spacious staircase and hall. And amid the real fleshly ills of cold and hunger, the forsaken child had found leisure to suffer still more from an imaginary evil: she was afraid of ghosts. The young man promised her protection against all ghosts whatsoever, and amusingly adds, "But, alas! I could offer her no other assistance." These two poor creatures, thin, starving, shivering, slept upon the floorboards with a bundle of law papers for a pillow, but with no other covering than a large horseman's cloak. They later discovered, in a garret, an old sofa cover, a small scrap of rug, and a few other fragments, which added a little to their warmth. In the night, the poor child crept close to him for warmth, and for security against her ghostly enemies. When he was not more than usually ill, he took her into his arms, and the child, warmed by this fraternal comfort, often slept when he could not. For, during the last two months of his sufferings, he slept much in the daytime, and was apt to fall into transient dozings at all hours. But his sleep was haunted by tumultuous dreams. He was often awakened suddenly. Pain and anguish began to violently disturb him as soon as he fell into a slumber, and, upon awakening, exhaustion carried him irresistibly back to it. What man of excitable and sensitive temperament has never known this *dog-sleep*, as the English language so elliptically terms it? For moral suffering will produce effects analogous to those produced by physical pains such as hunger. You can hear the sound of your own moans and are awakened suddenly by your own voice; your stomach, with convulsive motion, successively contracts and expands like a sponge being squeezed by a vigorous hand; your diaphragm constricts; your breathing is labored and your anguish multiplies, finding redress in the very intensity of the pain, until human nature explodes with a mighty cry that shakes your whole body, bringing about a violent deliverance.*

Meantime, the master of the house sometimes came in upon them suddenly, and very early; sometimes not till ten o'clock, and sometimes not at all. He was in constant fear of baliffs; and, improving on the plan of Cromwell, every night he slept in a different quarter of London, and examined, through a private window, the appearance of all those who knocked at the door. He breakfasted alone, with tea, rolls, or a few biscuits, never inviting a second person. During this marvelously frugal breakfast the young man generally contrived a reason for lounging into the room, and, with an air of as much indifference as he could assume, took up such fragments as had been left on the table—sometimes, indeed, there were none at all—all had been eaten. As for the poor girl, *she* was never admitted into his study, if one may so term such a jumbled mass of papers and parchments. At six o'clock this mysterious personage departed and locked up his room for the night. No sooner did he make his appearance the next morning, than the little girl was summoned below, where she resignedly assumed the duties of a menial servant. As soon as the man's hours of business commenced, the young vagabond went off to sit in the parks, or elsewhere, until nightfall. Then, when he returned to his desolate lair, his welcome knock sent the little girl running with trembling footsteps to the front door.

At a later epoch in his life, one August 15, at about ten o'clock in the evening, on his birthday, the author went to take a glance at the site of his former poverty. In the resplendent light of the beautiful front drawing-room, he observed a party, apparently cheerful and gay, assembled for tea—strange contrast to the darkness, cold silence, and desolation of that same house eighteen years before, when its nightly occupants were one famished student and an abandoned little girl. Later, he attempted to trace the poor child. Was she still living, perhaps with children of her own? He could never find her. He loved her as his partner in wretchedness, for she was neither pretty, nor pleasant, nor even intelligent. Plain human nature conciliated his affections, humanity reduced to its poorest expression. But, as I believe Robespierre expressed it in his passionate style of ice, melted and recast as abstraction: "Man never views man without pleasure!"

But who, and what, was the mysterious master of the house? He was one of those anomalous practitioners in lower departments of the law, of a type such as are found in all large cities who, engaged in intrigues and complex chicanery, had laid down his conscience for a time, meaning, doubtless, to resume this costly encumbrance as soon as he could afford it.* If he so wished, the author tells us, he could greatly amuse his readers at the expense of this sorry man, recounting strange scenes and inestimable episodes; but he wishes to forget everything save that this man, so despicable in other regards was, toward him, obliging; and, to the extent of his power, generous. The two children had as vast a choice of apartments as they could possibly desire for, except the paper-filled sanctuary, all other rooms were at their service and they could pitch their tent for the night in any spot they chose.

But the young man had another friend of whom it is now time to speak. The account he gives of this episode is, to my mind, so chaste and so full of grace, pity, and candor that, to do it justice, I would like, so to speak, to pluck a feather from an angel's wing. "From my earliest youth," says the author, "it has been my pride to converse familiarly, *more Socratico*, with all human beings— man, woman, and child—that chance might fling my way, a practice which is friendly to the knowledge of human nature, to good feelings, and to that frankness of address which becomes a man who would be thought a philosopher; for a philosopher should not see with the eyes of the poor limitary creature calling himself a *man of the world*, and filled with narrow and self-regarding prejudices, but should look upon himself as a *catholic* creature, and as standing in equal relation to high and low—to educated and uneducated, to the guilty and the innocent." Later, amid the favors granted by generous opium, we shall see this spirit of charity and universal fraternity reappear, but this time provoked and augmented by the singular genius of the intoxica- tion. In London, much more so than in Wales, the liberated student became a sort of peripatetic, a philosopher of the streets, continuously crossing and recrossing the great tumultuous city. The episode in question might seem misplaced in an English volume, for it is a fact that English literature is chaste to the point of prudery; but, to be sure, the same subject, had it been broached by a French pen, would have rapidly turned to the *shocking*,* whereas here it is treated with the greatest respect and decency. To sum all up in a word, our vagabond formed a platonic friendship with another order of peripatetic, a prostitute. Ann was not one of those bold, dazzling beauties, whose demon eyes glare at us through the mist, and who fashions a halo of her effrontery. Ann was a very simple, very ordinary girl, deprived and abandoned like so many others who, through betrayal, was reduced to a state of abjection. But she wore all the grace of youthful frailty and charity with which Goethe so skillfully clothes all of the female characters of his imagination, and which made an immortal being of his little Marguerite with the red hands.* On how many occasions during their monotonous peregrinations, pacing along interminable Oxford Street, through the swarming activity of the tumultuous city, had the famished student implored his unfortunate friend to seek the help of a magistrate against the miserable wretch who had robbed her, offering to speak in her behalf, with the contribution of his eloquent testimony! Ann was not as old as he; indeed, she had not yet completed her sixteenth year. How often had she taken his part against watchmen who wished to drive him off the steps of houses where he was seeking shelter! Once, she did even more, the poor girl. She and her friend were walking along Oxford Street, after a day when he felt more than usually ill. They turned off into Soho Square, and sat down on the steps of a house before which, the author avows, he could never again pass without feeling a pang of grief, and making an act of inner homage to the spirit of that unhappy generous girl. Suddenly, as they sat, he could sense his condition growing much worse. He had been leaning his head against the bosom of his sister in misfortune, and all at once he sank from her arms and fell backward on the steps. Without some powerful and reviving stimulus, he might have died on the spot, or might at least have sunk to a point of exhaustion from which he could never have recovered. Then it was, at the crisis of his fate, that his poor companion, who had herself met with little but injuries in this world, stretched out a saving hand to him. She uttered a cry of dismay and, without a moment's delay, ran off into Oxford Street. She soon returned with a glass of spiced port wine that acted upon his empty stomach, which would have rejected all solid food, with a marvelous and instantaneous power of restora-tion. "Oh! youthful benefactress! how often in succeeding years, standing in solitary places, and thinking of thee with grief of heart and perfect love, how often have I wished that, as in ancient times the curse of a father was believed to have a supernatural power, and to pursue its object with a fatal necessity of self-fulfilment—even so the benediction of a heart oppressed with gratitude might have a like prerogative; might have power given to it from above to chase, to haunt, to waylay, to overtake, to pursue thee into the central darkness of a London brothel, or (if it were possible) into the darkness of the grave, there to awaken thee with an authentic message of peace and forgiveness, and of final reconciliation!"

To feel this way, he must have suffered tremendously, his heart must have been of the sort that misfortune expands and makes tender, as opposed to those that it constricts and coarsens. The Bedouin of civilization learns, in the Sahara of the great cities, many modes of feeling which are beyond the comprehension of the man whose sensitivity is bounded by *home* and family. There is, in the *barathrum* of the capital cities, like in the desert, something which fortifies and shapes a man's heart, which fortifies it should he not deprave and weaken it to the point of abjection and suicide.*

One day, soon after this last incident, he chanced to meet, in

Albemarle Street, an old friend of his father's, who recognized him upon the strength of his family likeness. He answered all of the man's questions ingenuously, not attempting any disguise and, on his pledging that he would not betray him to his guardians, gave the man the address of his host, that most curious attorney. The next day he received from him a letter with a ten-pound bank note, which the attorney gave up to him honorably.

It might surprise the reader that the young man should not have found some means of staving off the extremes of poverty through the sources open to him, either to seek regular employ-ment or assistance from some family friend. As to the latter course, there would evidently be some danger, as what he dreaded most was the chance of being reclaimed by his guard-ians, and the powers with which they were invested by law would have allowed them fo forcibly restore him to the school he had quitted. Now, a force that is often found in the most feminine and sensitive natures gave him the courage to endure all of these dangers and privations rather than risk such a humiliating eventuality. Though his father had in his lifetime many friends in London, yet (as ten years had passed since his death) he remembered few of them, and fewer still by name. As for employment, he might doubtless have gained enough for his wants as a corrector of Greek proofs; such an office, he is sure, he could have discharged in an exemplary manner. But again, how was he to be introduced to a respectable publisher? At last, being absolutely candid, he admits that it had never once occurred to him to think of literary labors as a source of profit. No mode of obtaining money had ever entered his mind, save that of borrowing it on the strength of future claims, the fortune that he could expect from his inheritance. Finally, he introduced himself to a group of Jews whose shady dealings were handled by the attorney in question. He gave them an account of his expectations, which account, on examining his father's will at Doctors' Commons, they had ascertained to be correct. But one question still remained: Was *he* that person? To satisfy them, he produced some letters that he carried constantly in his pocket. When in Wales, he had received various letters from young friends; most of these were from the Earl of ＿＿,* dated from Eaton. Some also were from the Marquis of ＿＿,* the earl's father. The Jewish moneylenders at length deigned to furnish him with two or three hundred pounds, provided that he could persuade the young earl (who was, by the way, not older than himself) to guarantee the payment on their coming of age, their final object being, as he supposed, not the trifling profit he could expect to make, but the prospect of establishing a connection with his noble friend, whose immense expectations were well known. And thus, as soon as he had received the £10, our young vagabond prepared to go down to Eaton. Nearly £3 he had given to the moneylenders, for the preparation of the writings; a smaller sum he had given to his friend the attorney (who was connected to the money-lenders as their lawyer), to which he was entitled for his unfurnished lodgings; about fifteen shillings went to reestablish-ing his dress (what dress!); and of the remainder he gave one quarter to poor Ann. On a dark winter evening he set off, accompanied by the poor girl, for Piccadilly; for he intended to go down as far as Salt Hill on the Bristol mail. Having some time before them, they walked into Golden Square. There, near the corner of Sherrard Street, they sat down, not wishing to part in the tumult and blaze of Piccadilly. He now assured her that he would never forsake her and that he would come to her aid as soon as he could. In truth, this was a duty, even an imperious duty. He loved her as affectionately as a sister and, at that moment, with increased tenderness, from pity at witnessing her extreme dejection. Despite the shock his health had received, he was cheerful and full of hope, while Ann, on the contrary, was overcome by sorrow. At the moment of their final farewell, she threw her arms about his neck, and wept, without speaking a word. He hoped to return in a week, at furthest, and they agreed that on the fifth night from that, and every night afterward, she would wait for him at six o'clock, near the bottom of Great Titchfield Street, which had been their customary haven in the great Mediterranean of Oxford Street. This and other measures of precaution he took; one only he forgot. She had either never told him, or he had forgotten, as a matter of no great interest, her surname. It is a practice with these poor girls of humble rank to call themselves simply by their Christian names, *Mary, Jane, Frances*, etc., unlike those galant women of great pretentions, great readers of novels, who style themselves *Miss Douglas, Miss Montague*, etc. Moreover, as his final anxieties were spent in comforting Ann with hopes, and in pressing upon her the necessity of taking some medicines for a violent cough with which she was troubled, he wholly forgot to inquire after her surname, the surest means of tracing her thereafter in consequence of a missed meeting or a prolonged separation.

I must greatly abridge the account of his trip, which takes its tone from the charity and gentleness of a portly butler in the arms of whom our hero, overcome by exhaustion and the rocking movement of the train, cradled as if against a nurse's bosom— and by a long slumber in the open air between Slough and Eaton. For he had been obliged to retrace his steps on foot, having abruptly awakened in his neighbor's arms some six or seven miles past Salt Hill. Arriving at his destination, he learned that the young lord was no longer at Eaton. Unwilling to lose his journey, he called on Lord D____,* another old friend. His acquaintance with him, however, was not so intimate as with some others. Lord D____ invited him to a magnificent breakfast, the first regular meal he had sat down to for months. And yet he could scarcely eat anything. In London, on the day when he first received his bank note, he had gone to a bakery and bought two rolls. This very shop he had some weeks before surveyed with an eagerness of desire which it was almost humiliating for him to recollect.

But the bread that he so longed for had only made him ill, and this effect from eating he continued to feel for some weeks afterward. In the midst of all this luxury and comfort, his appetite vanished. He gave a short account of his sufferings to Lord D____, who called for wine. This afforded him a momentary pleasure.—As for the real object of his trip, the service which he had intended to ask of Lord ____ and which, by default, he instead had to ask of Lord D____, this he could not successfully complete. That is to say, Lord D____, who did not wish to mortify him by an absolute refusal, promised, after a little consideration, and under certain conditions, to give his security. Recomforted by this half-success, he returned to London, three days after he had left it. Unfortunately, the money-lenders did not approve of Lord D____'s terms. At this new crisis he would doubtlessly have relapsed into his former state of wretchedness, and at greater risk to himself this time, had not an opening been made, by dint of a chance he does not explain to us, for a reconciliation with his guardians, and had not this reconciliation changed his life. He left London in great haste and at length proceeded to the university. It was not until many months had passed that he had it in his power to revisit the scene of his youthful sufferings.

But what of poor Ann, what had become of her? He looked for her every day; he waited for her every night, at the corner of Titchfield Street. He inquired for her of everyone who might have known her; and, during the last hours of his stay in London, he employed every means of tracing her that the limited extent of his power made possible. The street where she had lodged he knew, but not the house; and he remembered at last some account which she had given of ill treatment from her landlord, which made it probable that she had quitted those lodgings before they had parted. Most people thought that the earnestness of his inquiries arose from dishonest motives, which moved their laughter, or their slight regard; and others, thinking he was in chase of a girl who had robbed him, were naturally indisposed to give him any clues to her. Finally, on the day he left London, he put his future address into the hands of the only person who knew her by sight. He never saw her again. This was, among such troubles as most men meet in life, his heaviest affliction. Note well that the worthy man who speaks thus is as commendable for the spirituality of his manners as for the nobility of his writings:

"If she lived, doubtless we must have been sometimes in search of each other, at the very same moment, through the mighty labyrinths of London, perhaps even within a few feet of each other—a barrier no wider than a London street, often amounting in the end to a separation for eternity! During some years I hoped that she *did* live; and I suppose that, on my different visits to London, I have looked into many myriads of female faces, in the hope of meeting her. I should know her again amongst a thousand if I saw her for a moment, for, though not handsome, she had a sweet expression of countenance and a peculiarly graceful carriage of the head. I sought her, I have said, in hope. So it was for years; but now I should fear to see her; and her cough, which grieved me when I parted with her, is now my consolation. Now I wish to see her no longer but think of her, more gladly, as one long since laid in the grave—in the grave, I would hope, of a Magdalen; taken away, before injuries and cruelty had blotted out and transfigured her ingenuous nature, or the brutalities of ruffians had completed the ruin they had begun.

"So then, Oxford Street, stony-hearted stepmother! thou that listenest to the sighs of orphans and drinkest the tears of children, at length I was dismissed from thee: the time was come at last that I no more should pace in anguish thy never-ending terraces; no more should dream and wake in captivity to the pangs of hunger. Successors too many to myself and Ann have, doubtless, since then trodden in our footsteps—inheritors of our calamities. Other orphans than Ann have sighed, tears have been shed by other children, and thou, Oxford Street, hast since, doubtless, echoed to the groans of innumerable hearts. For myself, however, the storm which I had outlived seemed to have been the pledge of a long fair weather..."

Is Ann, then, gone forever? Oh, no! we shall see her again through the worlds of opium, a strange and transfigured phantom, gradually assuming shape within the haze of memory, like the genie in the *Thousand-and-One Nights*, materializing out of the bottle's mist. As for the *opium-eater*, the calamities of his novitiate in London had struck root so deeply in his bodily constitution that afterward they shot up and flourished afresh, and grew into a noxious umbrage that overshadowed and darkened his latter years. And yet, these second assaults were met with a surer fortitude, with the resources of a maturer intellect, and with alleviations from sympathy and affection, how deep and how tender! These pages contain the noblest invocation, the gentlest expressions of grace addressed to his courageous companion, she who sat always by his bedside to bear him company through the heavy watches of the nights haunted by the Eumenides. The Orestes of opium has found his Electra, who, over the years, wiped away the unwholesome sweat from his forehead and refreshed his lips parched with fever. "For thou wast my Electra, dear companion of my later years! And neither in nobility of mind nor in long-suffering affection wouldst permit that a Grecian sister should excel an English wife!" And often-times, on moonlit nights, during his first mournful abode in

London, his consolation was (if such it could be thought) to gaze from Oxford Street up every avenue in succession which pierces through the heart of Marylebone to the fields and woods; and traveling with his eyes up the long vistas which lay part in light and part in shade, he said, "*That* is the road to the north and therefore to ____,* and if I had the wings of a dove, *that* way would I fly for comfort." A man like all others, blind in his desires! for in that very northern region it was, in that very valley, in that very house to which his wishes pointed, that the second birth of his sufferings began, in the company of a horde of ghastly phantoms. But there too dwells his consoling Electra. And now again he walked in London, a solitary and contemplative man, and again he paces the terraces of Oxford Street by night. And oftentimes, when he is oppressed by anxieties that demand all the sweet comfort of domestic support, he again looks up the streets that run northward from Oxford Street and dreams of his beloved Electra who awaits him in that very valley, in that very house. And the man cries, as the child once had done: "Oh, that I had the wings of a dove, *that* way would I fly for comfort!"

Here ends the prologue, and I can assure the reader, in all good faith, that the rising curtain will reveal nothing short of the most astonishing, most complex, and most splendid vision that the writer's fragile instrument has ever illuminated upon the snow-white page.

III. THE PLEASURES OF OPIUM

As I mentioned earlier, the author of these memoirs began to use opium as an article of daily diet for the purpose of mitigating a painful irritation of the stomach, which had been caused by his lamentable youthful adventures. That the irresistible desire to renew the mysterious excitement of his opium visions caused him to indulge in the frequent repetition of these exercises, this he does not deny, but rather confesses with great honesty, simply invoking the aid of an excuse. But his introduction to opium arose in the following way. From an early age he had been accustomed to washing his head in cold water at least once a day. Being suddenly seized with a toothache, which he attributed to some relaxation of the aforementioned daily regimen, he imprudently plunged his head into a basin of cold water, this time with dire consequences. With his hair thus wetted he went to sleep. He awoke with violent rheumatic pains of the head and face, from which he suffered for twenty days. On the twenty-first day, a rainy autumn Sunday of the year 1804, he went out into the streets of London to run away from his torments (he had returned to London for the first time since his entrance at the university) and met a school acquaintance who recommended opium. He took the tincture of opium in the quantity prescribed. That his pains had vanished was now a trifle in his eyes; this negative effect, which had previously loomed so large, was now swallowed up in the immensity of those positive effects which had suddenly opened up before him. What an upheaval of the spirit! What divine inner worlds! Was this, then, the panacea, the *pharmakon nepenthes** for all human woes?

"Here was the secret of happiness, about which philosophers had disputed for so many ages! Happiness might now be bought for a penny and carried in the waistcoat pocket; portable ecstasies might be had corked up in a pint bottle, and peace of mind could be sent down in gallons by mail coach! The reader will think I am laughing—I have a way of jesting at times in the midst of my own misery—but I can assure him that nobody will laugh long who deals much with opium: its pleasures even are of a grave and solemn complexion. And in his happiest state, the opium-eater cannot present himself in the character of *l'Allegro*; even then, he speaks and thinks as becomes *Il Penseroso*."*

The author is especially anxious to refute certain accusations directed against opium. It is not a sedative, at least not with respect to the intellect; it does not, and cannot, produce intoxication. As to laudanum, that might certainly intoxicate if a man could bear to take enough of it, but this is because it contains so much proof spirit, and not because it contains so much opium. He goes on to establish a comparison between the effects of alcohol and those of opium, and he clearly defines their differences. The pleasure given by wine is always mounting and tending to a crisis, after which it declines; that from opium, when once generated, is stationary for eight or ten hours. The first is a case of acute, the second of, chronic, pleasure. The one is a flame, the other a steady and equable glow. But the main distinction lies in this, that whereas wine disorders the mental faculties, opium, on the contrary, introduces among them the most exquisite order and harmony. Wine robs a man of his self-possession; opium renders this self-possession more supple and calm. True it is that wine gives a vivid exaltation to the contempts and admirations, the loves and hatreds of the drinker; opium, on the contrary, communicates serenity and divine repose to all the faculties. Men drunk on wine shake hands and shed tears, and no mortal knows why; there the sensual creature is clearly uppermost. But the expansion of the benigner feelings incident to opium is no febrile access; it is a healthy restoration of that state which the mind would naturally recover upon the removal of any bitterness that had disturbed and quarreled with the impulses of a noble temperament. But finally, however great its benefits, wine leads a man to the brink of absurdity and extravagance; and, beyond a certain point, is sure to volatilize and disperse the intellectual energies; whereas opium always seems to compose what had been agitated, and to concentrate what had been scattered. In short, a man who is drunk is in a condition which calls up into supremacy the merely human, too often the brutal part, of his nature. But the opium-eater feels that the nobler part of his nature is paramount, that the moral affections are in a state of cloudless serenity, and that over all is the great light of the majestic intellect.

The author also denies that the elevation of the spirits produced by opium is necessarily followed by a proportionate depression, and that the natural and even immediate consequence of opium is torpor and stagnation of the faculties. He assures the reader that for ten years, during which he took opium at intervals, the day succeeding to that on which he allowed himself this luxury was always a day of unusually good spirits. With respect to the torpor supposed to follow, or rather (if we were to credit the pictures of Turkish opium-eaters) to accompany, the practice of opium eating, he denies that also. Certainly, opium is classed under the head of narcotics, and some such effect it may produce in the end; but the primary effects of opium are always, and in the highest degree, to excite and stimulate the system. This first stage of its action lasts for upwards of eight hours, so that it must be the fault of the opium-eater himself if he does not so time his exposure to the dose as that the whole weight of its narcotic influence may descend upon his natural sleep. So that the reader may judge of the degree to which opium is likely to stupefy the faculties of an Englishman, the author shall, he says, by way of treating the question *illustratively*, rather than argumentatively, describe the way in which he himself often passed his *opium evenings* in London during the period between 1804 and 1812. He was then a diligent student and at severe studies for most of the time; and certainly he had, as he thought, as much right as anyone to occasionally relax in whatever manner he chose.

The late Duke of ____* used to say, "Next Friday, by the blessing of heaven, I propose to be drunk"; and in like manner, our author used to fix beforehand how often within a given time, and when, he would indulge in his favorite debauch. This was seldom more than once in three weeks, usually on a Tuesday or Saturday night, because these were his regular opera nights. This was during the time of the divine Grassini.* He heard the music, not as a simple succession of logical and pleasurable sounds, but like a collection of *memoranda,* like the accents of enchantment which displayed before his mind's eye the whole of his past life. Music interpreted and illuminated by opium—such was the nature of this intellectual debauch, the grandeur and intensity of which can be easily imagined by anyone possessed of a refined sensitivity. Many people ask what ideas can be attached to sounds; they forget, or rather are ignorant of the fact that music, in this respect twin to poetry, represents sentiments rather than ideas. Music suggests ideas—that is true enough—but it does not itself contain them. Music displayed before him the whole of his past life; not, he says, as if recalled by an act of memory, but as if present and incarnated in the sound; no longer painful to dwell upon, but the harsh detail of its incidents removed, or blended in some hazy abstraction, and its passions exalted, spiritualized, and ennobled. How many times must he witness, in this second theater, viewed through the luminous haze of opium, the mountain roads on which he rambled, a liberated student, and his kind hosts in Wales, and the London streets which lay part in light and part in shadow, and his lamentable friendships, and his long poverty, consoled by Ann and the hopes of a better future! And then through the gallery, in the intervals of the performance, the conversations of the Italian women and the music of the foreign language added all the more to the delight of the evening; for the less you understand of a language, the more sensitive you are to its harmony. Likewise, no one savors a landscape more than those who see it for the first time, nature then being revealed in all her strangeness, not yet having been dulled by too familiar a glance.

But another pleasure he had which, as it could be had only on a Saturday night, occasionally triumphed over his love for Italian opera. The pleasure in question, which struggled with his love of music, might be termed a charitable dilettantism. The author had been sorely and singularly tried, abandoned at a very young age to the indifferent uproar and din of the immense city. Even had his temperament not been of a virtuous, delicate, and affectionate sort, as the reader has no doubt noticed, we can readily imagine that he learned during his long days of wandering, and during his still longer nights of suffering, to love and pity the poor. The former student wished to revisit the humble life of the poor. He would dive into the very midst of the crowds and as the swimmer embraces the sea, thus entering into the most direct contact with nature, so he would, in a manner of speaking, take a bath among the disinherited masses. Here the tone of the book rises to such heights of eloquence that I cannot help but give the floor to the author himself:

"This pleasure, I have said, was to be had only on a Saturday night. What then was Saturday night to me more than any other night? I had no labors that I rested from, no wages to receive; what needed I to care for Saturday night, more than as it was a summons to hear Grassini? True, most logical reader, what you say is unanswerable. And yet so it was and is, that whereas different men throw their feelings into different channels, and most are apt to show their interest in the concerns of the poor chiefly by sympathy, expressed in some shape or other, with their distresses and sorrows, I at that time was disposed to express mine by sympathizing with their pleasures. The pains of poverty I had lately seen too much of, more than I wished to remember. But the pleasures of the poor, their consolations of spirit, and their reposes from toil, can never become oppressive to contemplate. Now, Saturday night is the season for the chief regular and periodic return of rest to the poor; in this point the most hostile sects unite and acknowledge a common link of brotherhood; almost all Christendom rests from its labors. It is a rest introductory to another rest and divided by a whole day and two nights from the renewal of toil. On this account I feel always, on a Saturday night, as though I also were released from some yoke of labor, had some wages to receive, and some luxury of repose to enjoy. For the sake, therefore, of witnessing, upon as large a scale as possible, a spectacle with which my sympathy was so entire, I used often, on Saturday nights, after I had taken opium, to wander forth, without much regarding the direction or distance, to all the markets, and other parts of London, to which the poor resort on a Saturday night for laying out their wages. Many a family party, consisting of a man, his wife, and sometimes one or two of his children, have I listened to, as they stood consulting on their ways and means, or the strength of their exchequer, or the price of household articles. Gradually I became familiar with their wishes, their difficulties, and their opinions. Sometimes there might be heard murmurs of discontent, but far oftener expressions on the countenance, or uttered in words, of patience, hope, and tranquillity. And taken generally, I must say that, in this point at least, the poor are far more philosophic than the rich—that they show a more ready and cheerful submission to what they consider as irremediable evils or irreparable losses. Whenever I saw occasion, or could do it without appearing to be intrusive, I joined their parties, and gave my opinion upon the matter in discussion, which, if not judicious, was always received indulgently. If wages were a little higher, or expected to be so, or the quartern loaf a little lower, or it was reported that onions and butter were expected to fall, I was glad; yet if the contrary were true, I drew from opium some means of consoling myself. For opium (like the bee, which extracts its materials indiscriminately from roses and from the soot of chimneys)* can overrule all feelings into compliance with the master key. Some of these rambles led me to great distances, for an opium-eater is too happy to observe the motion of time. And sometimes in my attempts to steer homeward upon nautical principles, by fixing my eye on the pole-star and seeking ambitiously for a *north-west passage* instead of circumnavigating all the capes and headlands I had doubled on my outward voyage, I came suddenly upon such knotty problems of alleys, such enigmatical entries, and such sphynx's riddles of streets without thoroughfares as must, I conceive, baffle the audacity of porters and confound the intellects of hackney coachmen. I could almost have believed, at times, that I must be the first discoverer of some of these *terræ incognitæ* and doubted whether they had been laid down in the modern charts of London. For all this, however, I paid a heavy price in distant years, *when the human face tyrannized over my dreams* and the perplexities of my steps in London came back and haunted my sleep, with the feeling of perplexities, moral or intellectual, that brought confusion to the reason, or anguish and remorse to the conscience.. ."

Thus opium does not of necessity produce inactivity or torpor; on the contrary, it often led our dreamer into the bustle of community life. Yet markets and theaters are not the appropriate haunts of the opium-eater, especially when in the divinest state incident to his enjoyment. In that state, crowds are an oppression to him; music even is too sensual and coarse. He naturally seeks solitude and silence as indispensable conditions of his raptures or deepest reveries. If at first the author of these *confessions* was drawn to seek the crowds and the moving currents of humanity, it was to avoid falling into a deep melancholy, from brooding too much on the sufferings he saw in his youth. Thus, to escape a sort of hypochondria, he forced himself into society and applied himself to the study of science. In after years, when his cheerfulness was more fully re-established, and the clouds of his former sufferings dispersed, he thought that he could yield to his inclination for a solitary life. More than once he spent an entire beautiful summer night sitting motionless close to an open window in a room from which he could overlook the sea below and could command a view of the great town, his thoughts deep in meditation and reveries suggested by the ravishing and peaceful scene that was spread before him like an allegory:

"The city, blurred by fog and glimmering evening lights, represented the earth, with its sorrows and its graves left behind, yet not out of sight nor wholly forgotten. The ocean, in everlasting but gentle agitation, and brooded over by a dove-like calm, might not unfitly typify the mind and the mood which then swayed it. For it seemed to me as if then first I stood at a distance and aloof from the uproar of life; as if the tumult, the fever, and the strife were suspended, a respite granted from the secret burdens of the heart, a Sabbath of repose, a resting from human labors. Here were the hopes which blossom in the paths of life, reconciled with the peace which is in the grave; motions of the intellect as unwearied as the heavens, yet for all anxieties a halcyon calm; a tranquillity that seemed no product of inertia, but as if resulting from mighty and equal antagonisms; infinite activities, infinite repose.

"Oh! just, subtle, and mighty opium!... thou hast the keys of Paradise...!"

Here then arise these unusual avowals, these testimonies of grace, which I have quoted at the beginning of this work and which could well serve as its epigraph. It is offered as the bouquet which closes the feast. For soon the scene will grow still and somber as storms gather in the night.

IV. THE TORTURES OF OPIUM*

He was introduced to opium for the first time in 1804. Eight pleasant years have passed, ennobled by study. We are now arrived at the year 1812. Far, very far away from Oxford, 250 miles away, in fact, buried in the depths of the mountains. And what is our hero (for surely he merits this title) doing now? Well, taking opium! Yes, but what else? He has been studying German metaphysics; reading Kant, Fichte, Schelling. Retired to a little cottage, with a single servant, he observes the calm and steady flow of the passing hours. And is he married? Not yet. And he still takes opium? On Saturday nights. And this diet has continued unblushingly since the famous "rainy Sunday" of 1804? Yes, even so! But how is his health after this long and regular debauch? He was never better in his life than in the spring of 1812, he tells us. Let us note that hitherto he had been only a dilettante eater of opium; and that opium had not yet become necessary to him as an article of daily diet. The doses were always taken in moderation, allowing intervals of several days between every indulgence. It was perhaps this prudence and moderation which delayed the drug's avenging terrors. But now comes a different era. Let us move on to the year 1813. In the preceding summer, he had suffered much in bodily health from distress of mind connected with a very melancholy event, which he does not explain.* So it was that in the year 1813 he was attacked by a most appalling irritation of the stomach, in all respects the same as that which had caused him so much suffering in his youth, so many nights of anguish in the most central recesses of the attorney's house, and which was accompanied by a revival of all the old dreams. Here at last is the great self-justification! What purpose would it serve to linger on this crisis and detail all of its events? The struggles were long, the suffering constant and insupportable, and the deliverance was always there, within easy reach. Here I take the liberty to say to all of you who are desirous of a balm, a palliative for your daily sorrows, you who have been troubled in the regular exercise of your lives and who have been drained of the last remnants of will, you who are sick in spirit and in body: Let he among you who is without sin, be it by action or be it by intention, cast the first stone at our author! This, then, is clear. Indeed, he goes on to ask us to believe that at the time he began to take opium daily, he could not have done otherwise. He could resist no longer. Are there so many brave men, after all, who are capable of encountering immediate pain and agony with unbounded energy and limitless hope, in the expectation of some vague, reversionary future benefit? He who appears so courageous and so patient does not in fact deserve any credit for winning a successful battle, whereas he who quickly gives in has actually expended immense energies in this short period of time, energies heretofore unbeknownst to himself. Are not human temperaments as infinitely varied as chemical quantums? "An *inhuman moralist* I can no more endure, in my nervous state, *than opium that has not been boiled!*" Here is a fine sentence, an irrefutable sentence. We must now consider extenuating circumstances rather than absolving ones.

The 1813 crisis did have a result, and one that could be easily foreseen. The reader is now to consider him as a regular and confirmed opium-eater, of whom to ask whether on any particular day he had or had not taken opium would be to ask whether *his lungs had performed respiration* or his *heart fulfilled its functions*. No Lent or Ramadan of abstinence from opium! Let us proceed forward by about three years. This year, 1816, was to be the most luminous, the happiest of his life, he tells us. He had, a little before this time, descended suddenly from 320 grains of opium (i.e., 8,000 drops of laudanum)* per day to 40 grains, thus diminishing his strange nourishment by seven-eighths. The cloud of profound melancholy which had rested upon his brain drew off in one day as if by magic, his intellectual agility returned, and he could once again believe in happiness; he now took only 1,000 drops of laudanum per day (what temperance!).

It was like an Indian summer for the intellect. And he read Kant again, and again understood him, or fancied that he did. Again his feelings of pleasure and joy expanded, feelings equally friendly to work and to fraternity. That outlook of benevolence and tolerance—let us go even further, of charity—toward one's fellow man, which bears some resemblance to the charity of drunkards (this mentioned with no intention of disrespect to so worthy an author), was set into strange and spontaneous motion one fine day, to the benefit of a Malay.—Remember this Malay, for we shall return to him later; he will reappear, amplified in a terrible manner. For who can calculate the reflective and repercussive force of such an incident, the images of which multiply in the dreamer's brain? Who can contemplate without a shudder the infinitely expanding circles in the wave of the intellect, agitated by a stone of chance?—So then, one day, a Malay knocked at the door of this still retreat. What business could a Malay have to transact among English mountains? He was, possibly, on his road to a seaport about forty miles distant. The servant who opened the door to him was born among those mountains and had never seen an Asiatic dress of any sort; his turban, therefore, confounded her not a little, and it turned out that *his* knowledge of English was exactly commensurate with *hers* of Malay. But the girl, recollecting the reputed learning of her master, and doubtless giving him credit for a knowledge of all the languages of the earth besides perhaps a few of the lunar ones, ran to tell him that there was a demon in the kitchen, whom she imagined that he could exorcise. A more striking picture there could not be imagined than the two gazing at each other: the face of the English girl, with her fair skin and independent attitude, contrasted with the mahogany skin of the Malay and his gestures of adoration; the one's face exquisitely fair, the other's sallow, with small, fierce, restless eyes. The scholar addressed the man in Greek, and he replied in what was probably Malay. In this way he saved his reputation with his servant and neighbors, for the Malay had no means of betraying the secret. He lay down upon the kitchen floor for about an hour and then, feeling more fit, pursued his journey. If the poor Asian had, as was likely, traveled on foot from London, it must have been nearly three weeks since he could have exchanged a word with any human being. In compassion for his solitary life our author, concluding that opium must be familiar to him as an Oriental, made him a gift, on his departure, of a large piece of the precious substance. Can a nobler manner of offering hospitality be conceived? The Malay, who, by the expression of his face, showed that he was familiar with opium, suddenly raised his hand to his mouth and bolted the whole, in a quantity enough to kill several men. He was, understandably, struck with some little consternation when he saw the result of this charitable gesture, but he never heard of any Malay being found dead on the main road and he became convinced that the strange traveler must have been sufficiently used to the poison and that he must have done him the service designed.

So then, as I have said, the opium-eater was still happy, knowing the true contentment of the scholar and solitary man who cherishes his *comfort*: a charming cottage, a handsome library, patiently and lovingly amassed, with winter raging without. Does not an attractive home render winter more poetic, and does not winter augment the poetry of the home? The white cottage sat at the foot of a small valley surrounded by mountains of a fair height and was embowered with flowering shrubs, so chosen as to spread a tapestry of flowers upon the walls, and clustering around the windows in a scented frame through all the months of spring, summer, and autumn, beginning with May roses, and ending with the jasmine. But the loveliest season, the most welcome season for a man given to dreams and meditation, is winter, winter in its harshest form. There are people who congratulate themselves when the winter is benign, and who are happy to see it go; but he, on the contrary, put up a petition anually for as much snow, hail, and frost as the sky could possibly deliver. He must have a Canadian winter or a Russian one for his money. Then his nest will be all the warmer, sweeter, and dearer: candles lit at four o'clock, a good fireplace, warm hearth rugs, thick curtains flowing in ample drapery to the floor, tea from eight o'clock at night to four o'clock in the morning, and a lovely woman to pour it. Without winter, none of these joys would be possible; all of these comforts require a very low temperature. Moreover, as our dreamer is called upon to pay heavily for these luxuries, he has the right to call upon winter to honestly pay *its* debt, as he paid his. The drawing-room is small, but being contrived to serve a double function, it is also, and more justly, termed the library, for there he has accumulated five thousand volumes, collected gradually, a truly patient victory. A great fire burns in the hearth. Upon the tea tray are placed two cups and two saucers, for his charitable Electra, whom he will introduce to us, brightened the cottage with all the sorcery of her angelic smiles. Why attempt to describe her beauty? The reader must surely understand that the power of her radiance is far from purely physical and that its portrayal lies beyond the means of any earthly brush. And, to be sure, let us not forget the flask of laudanum, a large decanter, good God! Because we are at a distance from London, and from all pharmacists as well. And next to it on the table lies a book of German metaphysics, witness to the eternal intellectual ambitions of its owner. Mountainous landscapes, silent retreats, luxury or rather solid well-being, vast leisure for meditation, harsh winter, just what is needed to concentrate the intellectual faculties; yes, it was certainly true happiness, or rather the last gleams of happiness, an intermittence in destiny, a jubilation amid misfortune. For now we are about to enter the hellish epoch when he must "bid farewell to sweet happiness, in winter or summer, farewell to smiles and laughter, farewell to hope and tranquil dreams, farewell to peace of mind and to the blessed consolations of sleep!" For more than three years, our dreamer will be as exiled from them, chased from the land of everyday happiness, for he is now arrived at an *Iliad of woes*; he now must record *the tortures of opium*. A period of melancholy thoughts, a vast veil of darkness, intermittently rent by rich and startling visions:

> —*As when some great painter dips*
> *His pencil in the gloom of earthquake and eclipse.**

These lines of Shelley, of a character so solemn and so truly Miltonic, impeccably render the hue of an opium landscape, if I may venture to speak in such terms. Here we find the mournful sky and melancholy horizons that suffocate the brain enslaved to opium. Infinities of horror and gloom and, above all, the inability to break free of these torturous bonds!

Before continuing, our penitent (we may from time to time call him by this name, even though he belongs, to all appearances, to that class of penitents who are always on the brink of relapsing into sin) warns that we will find no regular, connected shape in this section of the book, or at least no chronological order. When he wrote it, he was alone in London, incapable of constructing into a regular narrative the whole burden of horrors that lay upon his brain. He was exiled far from the friendly hands which customarily performed for him the offices of an amanuensis. He writes without precaution, almost without modesty from this point on, supposing himself writing to those who may be interested in him fifteen or twenty years later. And wishing simply to produce some record of this disastrous history, he does it as fully as he is able with the efforts he is capable of making, not knowing whether he can ever find time to do it again.

But why, the reader might ask, did he not release himself from the horrors of opium, by giving it up or by diminishing his daily ration? He did make innumerable attempts to reduce the quantity, but those who witnessed the agonies of those attempts were the first to beg him to desist. But could he not have reduced the quantity a drop a day, or by adding water, have bisected or trisected a drop? He calculated that a quantity of a thousand drops bisected would thus have taken nearly six years to reduce; and that way would have produced only an uncertain victory. Indeed, all those who know of opium experimentally know that down to a certain point it can be reduced with ease and even pleasure, but after that point, further reduction causes intense suffering. Yes, but why not suffer a little dejection for a few days? But no, there is nothing like low spirits. On the contrary, the mere animal spirits are uncommonly raised: the pulse is improved: the health is better. The suffering lies elsewhere. It is a state of unutterable irritation of stomach, accompanied by intense perspiration, born when the balance between physical energy and intellectual health is broken. Moreover, it is easy to understand that the body, that earthly part of man, which opium victoriously pacifies and reduces to a state of perfect submission, wishes to reclaim its dominion, while the empire of the intellect, which, until that point had been uniquely favored, finds itself even further diminished. It is an equilibrium that, once broken, seeks to be restored and which cannot any longer be restored without a crisis. Even discounting the stomach irritation and the excessive persperation, it is easy to imagine the anguish of a sensitive man, whose vitality is continually revived even while the intellect is disturbed and inactive. In this terrible situation, the afflicted will usually prefer the illness to the cure, and thus resigns himself to his destiny.

The opium-eater's studies have now been long interrupted. Yet he sometimes read aloud for the pleasure of others, for his wife and a young lady who came to drink tea with them; and at their request he would read Wordsworth's poems.* The more passionate poets he still read occasionally, but his proper vocation, the exercise of analytic understanding, he completely neglected. Philosophy and mathematics are continuous studies and not to be pursued by fits and starts, and these became insupportable to him. He now shrunk from them with a sense of powerless and infantile feebleness. A great work, to which he had dedicated his intellect and all of his energy, and to which he had given the title of an unfinished work of Spinoza's, from the *Reliquiœ—de Emendatione Humani Intellectûs*—was now lying, unfinished, on the mantlepiece with the desolate air of those great projects begun by overambitious governments or imprudent architects; and, instead of surviving him as a monument of wishes and aspirations, and a life of labor dedicated to the exaltation of human nature, it was now likely to stand a memorial to his presumption and defeated hopes. Fortunately he still had, for his amusement, political economy. And although it is eminently an organic science (no part, that is to say, but what acts on the whole, as the whole again reacts on each part), yet the several parts may be detached and contemplated singly. His wife sometimes read to him chapters from recent works of economy or parts of parliamentary debates, but for so erudite a literary man this was indeed a sad diet. Any man practiced in wielding logic might consider these the very dregs of the human intellect. Then, in 1819, a friend in Edinburgh sent him Mr. Ricardo's book,* and recurring to his own prophetic anticipation of the advent of some legislator for this science, he said, before he had finished the first chapter, "Thou art the man!" Wonder and curiosity were emotions that were reborn in him. Yet his greatest surprise lay in the fact that he could once again be stimulated to the effort of reading. His admiration for Mr. Ricardo was thus all the greater. Had this profound work really been written in nineteenth-century England? Thinking, he supposed, had become extinct in England. Mr. Ricardo had, at one stroke, introduced the law, constructed the base; he had thrown a ray of light over what had been but a shadowy collection of tentative discussions, a chaos in which all other writers before him had been lost. Our dreamer, the flame of inspiration burning bright, felt renewed, reconciled to intellectual activity and work, and began to write, or rather to dictate to his companion. It seemed to him that some important truths had escaped even the inevitable eye of Mr. Ricardo, the analysis of which, expressed by algebraic symbols, would provide material for an interesting little book. Great as was the prostration of his powers at that time, he nevertheless drew up his *Prolegomena to All Future Systems of Political Economy.*† Arrangements were made at a provincial press, about eighteen miles distant, for printing it. An additional compositor was retained for some days on this account. The work was even twice advertised, but alas! there was still the preface to write (the dreary task of writing a preface!) and a dedication, which he wished to make a splendid one, to Mr. Ricardo. What a trial for a mind debilitated by the ecstasies of a perpetual orgy! Oh, the humiliation of a nervous author, tyrannized by his internal atmosphere! He lies under the weight of his impotence, as terrible and insurmountable as polar ice. All of the arrangements were countermanded, the compositor dismissed, and his *Prolegomena* rested shamefully, peacefully by the side of its elder brother, the famous work suggested by Spinoza.

What a dreadful situation!* Your mind is crowded with ideas,

---

†Despite what De Quincey has said about his intellectual lethargy, this book, or something much like it, in which he treats the theories of Ricardo, was published posthumously. I refer the reader to the catalog* of his complete works.

and yet you are unable to cross the bridge that separates the imaginary land of dream from the real pastures of action! If you, reader, have ever known the necessities of production, you will sympathize with the despair of a noble, perspicacious, and clever intellect, wrestling with a damnation of the most personal kind. Abominable spell! Everything that I have already said in my study on hashish regarding the weakening of the will applies equally to the effects of opium. Answering a letter? A monumental undertaking, put off from hour to hour, from day to day. Finances? Puerile triviality. Domestic economy is then more neglected than political economy. If a mind debilitated by opium were wholly debilitated—if, to make use of the ignoble expression, it were to become completely besotted—the evil would evidently be less great or at least more tolerable. But an opium-eater loses none of his moral aspirations. He wishes and longs as earnestly as ever to realize what he believes possible and accomplish what he feels is required by duty; but his intellectual understanding of what is possible infinitely outruns his powers of execution. Execution? What am I saying? Does he have even the power to take the first step ? He lies under the weight of a nightmare that crushes both mind and body. Our poor man has now become a sort of Tantalus, longing to realize the duties he would fain perform, but as powerless as an infant to perform them; an intellect, a *pure intellect*, alas! condemned to desire that which he can never attain, a brave fighter rebuffed by all that he holds most dear, pinned under the incubus that forcibly confines him to his bed, where he consumes himself in impotent rage!

Thus the chastisement, slow and terrible, had come. Alas! intellectual torpor was not solely responsible, for there also intervened horrors of a nature more cruel and more real. The first symptom the opium-eater had of any important change going on in this part of his physical constitution was a curious one. It was the point of departure, the seed that would sow a succession of woes. Children are, in general, gifted with the singular power to perceive, or rather to create, upon the fertile canvas of darkness, a whole world of bizarre visions. In some, that faculty at times stirs without their having summoned it; others have a voluntary power to dismiss or summon such phantoms at will. In a like manner, our narrator found a reawakening of that childhood state. Already, toward the middle of 1817, this dangerous faculty cruelly tormented him. At night, when he lay awake in bed, vast processions passed mournfully before his eyes, friezes of never-ending stories, as sad and solemn as stories drawn from ancient times. But a sympathy arose between the waking and the dreaming states, so that the dreams of the sleeping state were very apt to transfer themselves to the dreams of the waking and whatsoever his eye evoked in the darkness was reproduced in his dreams with a disquieting, insupportable splendor. As Midas changed all things into gold,* and felt himself martyred by that ironic privilege, so the opium-eater saw all that he imagined in the darkness immediately shaped into inevitable realities in his dreams. And yet these spectacles, however beautiful and poetic they appeared, were accompanied by great torment and woe. He seemed every night to descend into sunless abysses, beyond all known depths, from which there seemed no hope of ever reascending. Nor did he, by waking, feel himself free of sadness, for the state of gloom which attended these gorgeous spectacles amounted at last to utter darkness, as of some suicidal despondency. By phenomena* analogous to those produced by hashish intoxication, the perception of space and, shortly afterward, the perception of time were curiously affected. Buildings and monuments were displayed in proportions so vast as were painful for the eye to behold. Space swelled and was amplified to an extent of unutterable infinity. But this was not so disturbing to him as the vast expansion of time. He sometimes seemed to have lived for a hundred years in one night. The minutest incidents of childhood, or forgotten scenes of later years, were often revived. If he had been told of them when waking, he would not have been able to acknowledge them as parts of his past experience. But placed as they were before him in dreams, he *recognized* them instantaneously, as a drowning man, at the very moment of supreme agony, will see the whole of his past life arrayed before him simultaneously as in a mirror; as a damned soul reads, in the space of a second, the terrible account of all of his earthly thoughts; as the stars that seem to withdraw before the common light of day are revealed when the obscuring daylight is withdrawn; as all inscriptions graven on the unconscious memory reappear, like writings traced in sympathetic ink.

The author *illustrates* the principal characteristics of his dreams with certain strange and impressive episodes. In one, especially, two very distant historical elements were juxtaposed in his mind in a most bizarre manner, according to the particular logic which governs the events of sleep. Thus, in the mind of a country gentleman revisiting his childhood, tragedy at times becomes the denouement of the comedy that had opened the play:

"I had been in youth, and even since, for occasional amusement, a great reader of Livy, whom, I confess, that I prefer, both for style and matter, to any other of the Roman historians; and I had often felt as most solemn and appalling sounds, and most emphatically representative of the majesty of the Roman people, the two words so often occurring in Livy, *Consul Romanus,* especially when the consul is introduced in his military character. I mean to say that the words *king, sultan, regent,* etc., or any other titles of those who embody in their own persons the collective majesty of a great people, had less power over my reverential feelings. I had also, though no great reader of history, made myself minutely and critically familiar with one period of

English history, the period of the Parliamentary War, having been attracted by the moral grandeur of some who figured in that day, and by the many interesting memoirs which survive those unquiet times. Both those parts of my lighter reading, having furnished me often with matter of reflection, now furnished me with matter for my dreams. Often I used to see, after painting upon the blank darkness a sort of rehearsal whilst waking, a crowd of ladies, and perhaps a festival and dances. And I heard it said, or I said to myself, 'These are English ladies from the unhappy times of Charles I. These are the wives and the daughters of those who met in peace, and sat at the same tables, and were allied by marriage or by blood; and yet, after a certain day in August 1642, never smiled upon each other again, nor met but in the field of battle; and at Marston Moor, or at Newbury, or at Naseby, cut asunder all ties of love by the cruel saber and washed away in blood the memory of ancient friendship.' The ladies danced and looked as lovely as at the court of George IV. Yet I knew, even in my dream, that they had been in the grave for nearly two centuries. This pageant would suddenly dissolve; and, at a clapping of hands, would be heard the heart-quaking sound of *Consul Romanus*; and immediately came sweeping by, in gorgeous paludaments, Paulus or Marius, girt round by a company of centurions, with the crimson tunic hoisted on a spear, and followed by the frightful cry of the Roman legions."

Astonishing and monstrous architecture rose up in his dreams, similar to those shifting abstractions envisioned by the eye of a poet in the colored clouds of a setting sun. But soon these dreams of terraces, courts, and ramparts, lifting up to unimaginable heights and sinking far into wondrous depths, gave way to visions of lakes and vast stretches of water. Water then was the focus of an obsession. We have already remarked, in our study of hashish, the mind's amazing predilection for the liquid element and its mysterious seductions. Have we not reported a unique relationship between the two stimulants, at least in their effects upon the imagination or, if one prefers this explanation, that the human mind, under the sway of a stimulant, is more likely to be attracted to certain images? The waters now changed their character—from translucent lakes, shining like mirrors, they now became seas and oceans. And then a new metamorphosis made of these magnificent waters, disquieting by their frequency and their range, an abiding torment. Our author had been too enamored of crowds, had plunged too deliciously into the sea of the multitudes, for the human face not to have played a despotic part in his dreams. And now that which he has called, I believe, the *tyranny of the human face** began to unfold itself. "Now it was that upon the rocking waters of the Ocean the human face began to appear: the sea appeared paved with innumerable faces, upturned to the heavens; faces, imploring, wrathful, despairing, surged upward by thousands, by myriads, by generations, by centuries. My agitation was infinite, my mind tossed and surged with the Ocean."

The reader will have already remarked that for some time, the man has not summoned the images, but rather the images have appeared of their own volition, spontaneously, despotically. He cannot now dismiss them, for the will has been enfeebled and can no longer govern the faculties. The poetic memory, heretofore a source of infinite pleasure, has become an inexhaustible arsenal of torturous instruments.

In 1818, the Malay of whom we have already spoken returned to torment him cruelly; he was now an intolerable visitor. Like space and time, the Malay was amplified. He came to represent all of Asia; ancient Asia, as solemn, monstrous and complicated as its temples and its religions; where everything, from the most ordinary habits of everyday life to the most grandiose and elaborate memories connected with it, is so contrived as to confound the European mind. And it was not only China, bizarre and artificial, as prodigious and antiquated as a fairy tale, which terrified him. From kindred feelings, he naturally recalled the neighboring image of India, so mysterious and disturbing to the Western mind; and soon China and India combined with Egypt to form a menacing triad, a complex nightmare of astonishing horror. Briefly, the Malay had evoked the entire immense and fabulous Orient. The pages that follow are too lovely to abridge:

"I have been every night, through his means, transported into Asiatic scenes. I know not whether others share in my feelings on this point; but I have often thought that if I were compelled to forgo England, and to live in China, and among Chinese manners and modes of life and scenery, I should go mad. The causes of my horror lie deep, and some of them must be common to others. Southern Asia, in general, is the seat of awful images and associations. As the cradle of the human race, it would alone have a dim and reverential feeling connected with it. But there are other reasons. No man can pretend that the wild superstitions of savage tribes anywhere in the world affect him in the way that he is affected by the ancient, monumental, cruel, and elaborate religions of Indostan, etc. The mere antiquity of Asiatic things, of their institutions, histories, modes of faith, etc., is so impressive that to me the vast age of the race and name overpowers the sense of youth in the individual. A young Chinese seems to me an antediluvian man renewed. Even Englishmen, though not bred in any knowledge of such institutions, cannot but shudder at the mystic sublimity of castes that have flowed apart, and refused to mix, through such immemorial tracts of time; nor can any man fail to be awed by the names of the Ganges or the Euphrates. It contributes much to these feelings that Southern Asia is, and has been for thousands of years, the part of the earth most swarming with human life, the great *officina gentium*. Man is a weed in those regions. The vast empires also, in which the enormous population of Asia has always been cast, give a further sublimity to the feelings associated with all Oriental names or images. In China, over and above what it has in common with the rest of Southern Asia, I am terrified by the modes of life, by the manners, and the barrier of utter abhorrence, and want of sympathy placed between us by feelings deeper than I can analyze. I could sooner live with lunatics or brute animals. All this, and much more than I can say, or have time to say, the reader must enter into before he can comprehend the unimaginable horror which these dreams of Oriental imagery and mythological tortures impressed upon me. Under the connecting feeling of tropical heat and vertical sunlight, I brought together all creatures, birds, beasts, reptiles, all trees and plants, usages and appearances that are found in all tropical regions, and assembled them together in China or Indostan. From kindred feelings, I soon brought Egypt and all her gods under the same law. I was stared at, hooted at, grinned at, chattered at, by monkeys, by parrots, by cockatoos. I ran into pagodas, and was fixed for centuries at the summit, or in secret rooms; I was the idol; I was the priest; I was worshiped; I was sacrificed. I fled from the wrath of Brama through all the forests of Asia; Vishnu hated me; Siva laid wait for me. I came suddenly upon Isis and Osiris: I had done a deed, they said, which the ibis and the crocodile trembled at. I was buried for a thousand years in stone coffins, with mummies and sphinxes, in narrow chambers at the heart of eternal pyramids. I was kissed with cancerous kisses by crocodiles and laid, confounded with all unutterable slimy things, amongst reeds and Nilotic mud.

"I thus give the reader some slight abstraction of my Oriental dreams, which always filled me with such amazement at the monstrous scenery that horror seemed absorbed, for a while, in sheer astonishment. Sooner or later came a reflux of feeling that swallowed up the astonishment and left me not so much in terror as in hatred and abomination of what I saw. Over every form, and threat, and punishment, and dim sightless incarceration brooded a sense of eternity and infinity that drove me into an oppression as of madness. Into these dreams only, it was, with one or two slight exceptions, that any circumstances of physical horror entered. All before had been moral and spiritual terrors. But here the main agents were ugly birds, or snakes, or crocodiles, especially the last. The cursed crocodile became to me the object of more horror than almost all the rest. I was compelled to live with him, and (as was almost always the case in my dreams) for centuries. I escaped sometimes and found myself in Chinese houses with cane tables, etc. All the feet of the tables, sofas, etc., soon became instinct with life: the abominable head of the crocodile, and his leering eyes, looked out at me, multiplied into a thousand repetitions, and I stood loathing and fascinated. And so often did this hideous reptile haunt my dreams that many times the very same dream was broken up in the very same way: I heard gentle voices speaking to me (I hear everything when I am sleeping) and instantly I woke; it was broad noon and my children were standing, hand in hand, at my bedside, come to show me their colored shoes, or new frocks, or to let me see them dressed for going out. I protest that so awful was the transition from the damned crocodile, and the other unutterable monsters and abortions of my dreams, to the sight of innocent *human* natures and of infancy that, in the might and sudden revulsion of mind, I wept, and could not forbear it, as I kissed their faces."

The reader might expect to see, echoing within this gallery of bygone memories, the melancholic countenance of poor Ann. She will have her turn. The author remarks that the deaths of those whom we love, and indeed the contemplation of death generally, is more affecting in summer than in any other season of the year. And the reasons are these three: first, that the heavens in summer appear far higher, more distant, and (if such a solecism may be excused) more infinite; the clouds, by which chiefly the eye expounds the distance of the blue pavilion stretched over our heads, are in summer more voluminous, massed, and accumulated in far grander and more towering piles; secondly, the light and the appearances of the declining and the setting sun are much more fitted to be types and characters of the infinite; And thirdly, which is the main reason, the exuberant and riotous prodigality of life naturally forces the mind more powerfully upon the antagonist thought of death, and the wintry sterility of the grave. For it may be observed, generally, that wherever two thoughts stand related to each other by a law of antagonism and exist, as it were, by mutual repulsion, they are apt to suggest each other. The author also confesses that he finds it impossible to banish the thought of death when he is walking alone in the endless days of summer; and any particular death, if not more affecting, at least haunts his mind more obstinately and besiegingly in that splendid season.

He dreamed that it was a Sunday morning in May; that it was Easter Sunday, and as yet was very early in the morning. It seemed to him as if he stood at the door of his own cottage. Right before him lay the very scene which could really be commanded from that situation, but exalted, as was usual, and solemnized by the power of dreams. There were mountains and the same lovely valley at their feet, but the mountains were raised to more than Alpine height, and there was interspace far larger between them of meadows and forest lawns. The hedges were rich with white roses, and no living creature was to be seen, excepting that in the green churchyard there were cattle tranquilly reposing upon the verdant graves, and particularly round about the grave of a child whom he had tenderly loved, just as the author had really beheld them, a little before sunrise in the same summer, when that child died. He told himself then, "It yet wants much of sunrise, and it is Easter Sunday, and that is the day on which they celebrate the first fruits of resurrection. I will walk abroad; old griefs shall be forgotten today, for the air is cool and still, and the hills are high, and stretch away to heaven; and the forest glades are as quiet as the churchyard; and with the dew I can wash the fever from my forehead, and then I shall be unhappy no longer." He turned, as if to open his garden gate, and immediately saw upon the left a scene far different. The scene was an Oriental one; and there also it was Easter Sunday, and quite early in the morning. And at a vast distance were visible, upon the faint horizon, the domes and cupolas of a great city (an image caught perhaps in childhood from some picture of Jerusalem). Not far from him, upon a stone, and shaded by Judean palms, sat a woman. It was Ann!

"She fixed her eyes upon me earnestly, and I said to her at length, 'So then I have found you at last!' I waited: but she answered me not a word. Her face was the same as when I saw it last, and yet again how different! Seventeen years ago, when the lamplight fell upon her face, as for the last time I kissed her lips (lips, Ann, that to me were not polluted), her eyes were streaming with tears. The tears were now wiped away; she seemed more beautiful than she was at that time, but in all other points the same, and not older. Her looks were tranquil, but with unusual solemnity of expression; and I now gazed upon her with some awe, but suddenly her countenance grew dim, and turning to the mountains, I perceived vapors rolling between us; in a moment, all had vanished, thick darkness came on, and in the twinkling of an eye I was far away from the mountains, and by lamplight in Oxford Street, walking again with Ann—just as we walked seventeen years before, when we were both children."

The author cites another specimen of his morbid dreams, and this final one (which dates from 1820) is all the more terrible for being more vague, of a nature more rare and fleeting; and, charged as it is with poignant feeling, it reveals and multiplies the continually shifting forms of the indefinite. I despair of conveying to the reader the magic of the English style:

"The dream commenced with a music which now I often heard in dreams—a music of preparation and of awakening suspense, a music like the opening of the Coronation Anthem and which, like that, gave the feeling of a vast march, of infinite cavalcades filing off and the tread of innumerable armies. The morning was come of a mighty day, a day of crisis and of final hope for human nature, then suffering some mysterious eclipse and laboring in some dread extremity. Somewhere, I knew not where—somehow, I knew not how—by some beings, I knew not whom—a battle, a strife, an agony was conducting, was evolving like a great drama or piece of music with which my sympathy was the more insupportable from my confusion as to its place, its cause, its nature, and its possible issue. I, as usual in dreams (where, of necessity, we make ourselves central to every movement), had the power, if I could raise myself, to will it; and yet again had not the power, for the weight of twenty Atlantics was upon me, or the oppression of inexpiable guilt. 'Deeper than ever plummet sounded,'* I lay inactive. Then, like a chorus, the passion deepened. Some greater interest was at stake, some mightier cause than ever yet the sword had pleaded or trumpet had proclaimed. Then came sudden alarms, hurryings to and fro, trepidations of innumerable fugitives—I knew not whether from the good cause or the bad. Darkness and lights, tempest and human faces, and at last, with the sense that all was lost, female forms, and the features that were worth all the world to me,. and but a moment allowed—and clasped hands, and heartbreaking partings, and then—everlasting farewells! And with a sigh, such as the caves of hell sighed when the incestuous mother uttered the abhorred name of death, the sound was reverberated—everlasting farewells! And again, and yet again reverberated—everlasting farewells!

"And I awoke in struggles, and cried aloud, 'I will sleep no more!'"*

V. A FALSE DENOUEMENT

De Quincey shortened the conclusion of his book in the most singular manner, or so it originally seemed to me. I remember that when I read it for the first time, already many years ago (and I was not then familiar with the *Suspiria de Profundis*, which, indeed, had not yet been published), I said to myself from time to time: What possible denouement could such a book have? Death? Madness? But the author, speaking always in his personal voice, was evidently in a state of health which, if not absolutely normal and excellent, nevertheless allowed him to devote his efforts to his literary work. What seemed to me the most likely, was the *status quo*; that he grew accustomed to his pain, and that he internalized the alarming effects of his bizarre habit. I said to myself then: Robinson, at last, left his island; a boat can pull away from the shore, and so be restored to solitary exile; but what man can quit the empire of opium? Thus, I reasoned further, this curious book, whether it be truthful confession or pure invention (the latter hypothesis being improbable because of the truthful lustre that pervades the entire work and the inimitable tone of sincerity that accompanies each detail), is without a denouement. Obviously, some books, such as tales of adventure, have no denouement. They deal with eternal themes, and everything that relates to the irremediable, to the irreparable, belongs to this category. Yet I recalled that the opium-eater had somewhere in the beginning of his work announced that he had untwisted, link by link,* *the accursed chain which fettered him.* Therefore, the conclusion was, for me, completely unexpected; and I can honestly state that when I first read it, despite the whole apparatus of detailed realism, I instinctively mistrusted it. I do not know whether the reader shares my impression in this regard, but I will say that the subtle, ingenious manner by which the unfortunate man quit the enchanted labyrinth in which, through his own fault, he was lost, seems to me an invention typical of a certain sort of British *tale,* a sacrifice in which truth is laid aside in deference to public modesty or prejudice. We recall the many precautions with which he prefaced the beginning of the narrative of his *Iliad of woes,* and how carefully he established the right to draw up his *confessions;* how he hoped that they would even prove to be useful. Some people will yearn for *moral* denouements and others for *consoling* ones. Thus women, for example, never wish to see miscreants rewarded. What would our theater audiences say if, at the end of the fifth act, they were not treated to the catastrophe which restores the normal, or rather utopian, equilibrium among all of the parties as justice demands—that equitable catastrophe awaited so impatiently during all of those four long acts? In brief, I think that the public holds *impenitents* in low regard and tends to view them as *insolents.* De Quincey might have thought the same and acted accordingly. If these pages, written earlier, had by chance come to his attention, I imagine that he would have deigned to smile complacently at my early, justifiable mistrust. In any event, I rely on his text, so penetrating and so sincere on all other occasions, and I can already report here a certain *third prostration before the dark idol** (which implies a second) of which we shall have something to say in a few moments.

Whatever the case, here is the denouement. Opium had long since ceased to found its empire on spells of pleasure; it was solely by the tortures connected with the attempts to abjure it that it kept its hold, and these tortures (which are perfectly believable and in accord with all experiences relative to the difficulties of breaking long-time habits, of whatever type) had begun with his very first efforts to break free of that daily tyranny. Between two agonies—the one from continued use and the other from interruption of a daily regimen—the author preferred, he tells us, to choose the path that held out the hope of deliverance. "How much I was at that time taking I cannot say; for the opium which I used had been purchased for me by a friend who afterward refused to let me pay him, so that I could not ascertain even what quantity I had used within the year. I apprehend, however, that I took it very irregularly and that I varied from about fifty or sixty grains to 150 a day. My first task was to reduce it to forty, to thirty, and as fast as I could to twelve grains." He adds that of all the medicines he tried, he derived no benefit from any except one, ammoniated tincture of valerian. But why trouble the reader (says the author) with a continued narrative of his convalescence and cure? The object of the book was to display the marvelous agency of opium, whether for pleasure or for pain. That done, the book has reached its conclusion. The moral of the narrative addresses only opium-eaters. Let them learn to fear and tremble; let them know, through this extraordinary example, that opium, after seventeen years' use and eight years' abuse, can be renounced. May they, the author adds, bring to the task greater energy and attain the same success!

"Jeremy Taylor* conjectures that it may be as painful to be born as to die. I think it probable, and during the whole period of diminishing the opium, I had the torments of a man passing out of one mode of existence into another. The issue was not death, but a sort of physical regeneration. And I may add that ever since, at intervals, I have had a restoration of more than youthful spirits, though under the pressure of difficulties which, in a less happy state of mind, I should have called misfortunes.

"One memorial of my former condition still remains. My dreams are not yet perfectly calm; the dread swell and agitation of the storm have not wholly subsided; the legions that encamped in them are drawing off, but not all departed; my sleep is still tumultuous, and, like the gates of Paradise to our first parents when looking back from afar, it is still (in the tremendous line of Milton),

With dreadful faces throng'd and fiery arms.*

The appendix,* which dates from 1822, is intended to more meticulously corroborate the credibility of the denouement—to give, so to speak, a medical account of his emancipation. To descend from so large a quantity as 8,000 drops to so small a one as ranging between 300 and 160 drops is certainly a magnificent triumph. But the effort which remained called for far more energy than he had anticipated, and the necessity for making it was ever more apparent. He especially noticed an increasing callousness or defect of sensitivity in the stomach, which seemed to portend a scirrhous state of that organ. The physician informed him that the continued use of opium, even in reduced quantities, could certainly lead to such an outcome. From then on, he resolved to renounce it completely. The account of his efforts, his hesitations, and the physical hardships he suffered, at the time of his first triumphs of will, is truly interesting. He reduced his daily quantum of opium; twice he arrived at zero. Then there were relapses, during which he often made up for the previous abstinences. Meantime, the experience of the first six weeks led to an enormous irritability and excitement throughout his system. His stomach in particular was restored to a normal vitality but often caused him great pain and unceasing restlessness night and day. Sleep (what sleep!)—three hours out of the twenty-four was the most he had, and that so agitated and shallow that he heard every sound near him. His lower jaw swelled constantly; his mouth was ulcerated. And he had many other symptoms of a more or less deplorable nature, including violent sternutation, which became exceedingly troublesome, sometimes lasting for two hours and recurring at least twice or three times a day. Then a violent cold attacked him, and a cough soon after, something that had never once happened during the whole period of years through which he had taken opium. Through taking bitters, the healthy state of his stomach was restored—that is to say, like other men, his process of digestion again operated, as it had formerly, below consciousness. On the forty-second day the symptoms already noticed began to retire and new ones to arise of a different and far more tormenting class, but he did not know whether they were the consequences of his former abuse of opium or from its want. And it so happened that the excessive perspiration, which even at Christmas attends any great reduction in the daily quantum of opium had, in the hottest season, wholly retired. But other symptoms could be attributed to the dampness, which had about that time attained its maximum, July having been a month of incessant rain in the most rainy part of England.

The author goes to the trouble (always for the sake of those unfortunate souls who might find themselves in the same situation) of giving us a synoptic table, with the dates and quantities, of the first five weeks during which he set his plan in glorious motion. The table reveals terrible relapses, as when he ascended from zero to 200, 300, 350 drops. But perhaps the decrease was too rapid, or not sufficiently graduated, thus leading him to seek, in the very source of his affliction, relief from the needless suffering.

The scoffing, teasing, and even bantering tone that pervades much of the appendix strongly confirms my idea that the conclusion is at least partially *artificial*. Finally, to demonstrate that the attentions he bestows on such a miserable body as his own are not those of a self-serving valetudinarian, and to punish it for having so tormented him, the author calls down upon his contemptuous body the treatment which the law inflicts upon the bodies of the worst malefactors. And if the physicians of

London believe their science can reap any benefit from inspecting the body of such a devoted opium-eater, he will readily bequeath them his own. There was once a Roman prince who, upon notification made to him by rich persons that they had left him a handsome estate in their wills, used to express his entire satisfaction at such arrangements, and his gracious acceptance of these loyal legacies; but then, if the testators neglected to give him immediate possession of the property, if they traitorously "persisted in living," as Suetonius pleasantly expresses it, he was highly provoked, and took his measures accordingly. In those times, and from one of the worst Caesars, we might expect such conduct, but the opium-eater is sure that from English surgeons he need look for no such shocking expressions of impatience, or of any other feelings, but such as are answerable to that pure love of science and all its interests, which induces him to make such an offer of his precious remains. May this legacy be infinitely postponed. May this remarkably insightful writer, this afflicted man, so charming even in his mockeries, stay with us longer even than did the fragile Voltaire, who, as they say, took eighty-four years to die!†

---

†As we write these lines, the news of the death of Thomas De Quincey has reached Paris. We wish, then, for the continuation of that glorious destiny which was so brusquely shortened. The worthy follower and friend of Wordsworth, Charles Lamb, Hazlitt, and Wilson has left us with a great number of works, * the principal of which are *Confessions of an English Opium-Eater; Suspiria de Profundis; The Caesars; Literary Reminiscences; Essays on the Poets; Autobiographic Sketches; Memorials; The Notebook; Theological Essays; Letters to a Young Man; Classic Records Reviewed or Deciphered; Speculations, Literary and Philosophic, with German Tales and Other Narrative Papers; Klosterheim, or the Masque; Logic of Political Economy* (1844); *Essays Skeptical and Antiskeptical on Problems Neglected or Misconceived,* etc. He leaves a reputation not only as one of the most original, truly humorous minds of old England, but also as one of the most affable, charitable characters ever to honor the history of letters, as he shows in the *Suspiria de Profundis,* which we shall attempt to analyze. The

VI. THE CHILD GENIUS

The *Confessions* dates from 1822, and the *Suspiria*,* which forms their continuation and complement, was written in 1845. Consequently, the tone of the latter is, if not completely different, at least more serious, more melancholy, more resigned. Time and again, as I examined these unique pages, I could not

---

title of this work lends to this painful circumstance a sense of intensified melancholy. Mr. De Quincey died at Edinburgh at the age of seventy-five.

I have before me an obituary notice* dated 17 December 1859, which provides material for sad reflection. From one end of the world to the other, the great madness of morality usurps the place of pure literature in all discussions. The Pontmartins* and other drawing-room preachers clutter American and British newspapers as well as our own. I have already had the opportunity to observe, in connection with the strange funeral rites that followed the death of Edgar Allan Poe, that the burial ground of literature is less respected than the common graveyard, where a bylaw protects the graves against the *innocent* outrages of animals.

I would have the impartial reader be the judge. If the *opium-eater* never rendered *positive services to humanity*, what could it matter to us? If his book is *beautiful*, we owe him gratitude. Did not Buffon (who is not suspect on a similar subject) think that for the truly thoughtful man, a skillful quip or a new manner of turning a phrase was more useful than the discoveries of science—in other words, that Beauty is nobler than Truth?*

If De Quincey at times showed himself to be unusually harsh toward his friends, what author, knowing the ardor of literary passion, could justifiably be astonished? He had cruelly mistreated himself, and, indeed, as he somewhere said, and as Coleridge said before him, "Malice is not always of the heart; there is a malice of the understanding and the fancy."*

But here we have the critic's masterpiece. In his youth, De Quincey had made a gift to Coleridge of a considerable part of his inheritance*: "this was surely noble and laudable, *albeit imprudent*," said the English biographer, "but one must remember that there came a time when, victim to his opium, his health debilitated and his affairs thrown into disorder, he was perfectly willing to accept the charity of his friends." If our translation is correct, this would mean that he should not be given credit for his generosity, since he later accepted that of others. Genius does not acknowledge such traits. In order to rise to such heights, a man must be gifted with the envious, mean spirit of the moral critic.

help thinking of the various metaphors that poets have used to portray the man who has survived his battles with life. Here is an old sailor, his back bent, his face etched with a lattice of inextricable lines, returning to his distant home to revive a heroic body that has escaped a thousand perils; here is a traveler who, many an evening, walks back over the lands he had crossed in the morning, thinking with wistfulness and sorrow of the thousand fancies he had nurtured as he sees them vanishing on the horizon. It is that which, in a general manner, I shall venture to call a *spectral* tone—not supernatural but almost beyond the human, half terrestrial and half otherworldly. It is a tone which we find at times in *Mémoires d'outre-tombe*,* when the great René, having stilled his anger or wounding pride, finds that an uncomplaining apathy has displaced the scorn he had formerly felt for earthly things.

The "Introductory Notice" to the *Suspiria* informs us that the opium-eater, despite all the heroism he was able to summon for his patient cure, succumbed to a second and then a third relapse. This is what he terms "a third prostration before the dark idol." Even omitting the physiological reasons he pleads as his excuse, as for example having failed to supervise his abstinence with sufficient prudence, I believe that this misfortune was easy enough to foresee. But this time it is no longer a question of struggle or rebellion. Struggle and rebellion always imply a certain degree of hope, whereas despair is mute. There, where remedy is impossible, lie the greatest sufferings. The doors, once held open for the return voyage, are now tightly shut, and man walks docilely forward to meet his destiny. *Suspiria de Profundis!* This book is appropriately titled.

The author does not here insist, as he had before, that his *Confessions* were written for the good of the public health. The *Confessions* were written, he frankly tells us, with some purpose of exposing the specific power of opium upon the natural faculty of dreaming. To dream magnificently is not a gift accorded to all men, and even among those who possess it, it is at serious risk of being ever more diminished by steadily growing modern dissipation and by the turbulence of material progress. The faculty for dreaming is divine and mysterious, for it is through dreams that man communicates with the shadowy world that surrounds him. But that faculty must have solitude to develop freely; the more man retires in thought, the more apt he is to dream freely and deeply. And what solitude is greater, calmer, further separated from the world of earthly interests than that created by opium?

The *Confessions* presented the record of the youthful incidents which served to explain and justify his use of opium. But until this moment there have been two important lacunae. One is composed of the dreams engendered by opium during the author's stay at the university (which he terms his "Oxford Visions"); the other of the narratives of his childhood impressions. Thus in the second section as in the first, the biography will explain and "verify," so to speak, the mind's mysterious adventures. It is within these notes relative to childhood that we find the seed of the strange dreams of the adult man and, furthermore, of his genius. Every biographer has understood, more or less thoroughly, the importance of anecdotes in connection with the childhood of the writer or artist. But I find that this important point has never been sufficiently acknowledged. Often, in thinking about works of art—not in their easily grasped material sense nor in the obvious hieroglyphics of their contours nor yet in the evident sense of their subjects, but rather in the soul with which they are endowed, in the atmospheric impressions they render, in the light or the spiritual shade they throw upon our souls—I have been struck by something like a vision of their author's childhood. This little sorrow, that little childhood delight, immeasurably amplified by an exquisite sensitivity, will later become, in the adult man, and even without his knowledge, the basis for a work of art. Finally, to explain my meaning in a more precise manner, would it not be easy to prove, by a philosophical comparison between the works of a mature artist and the state of his soul when he was a child, that genius is but childhood clearly expressed, now gifted with the ability to communicate in a virile and powerful voice? And yet, I do not presume to deliver this psychological idea as anything more than pure conjecture.

We will rapidly analyze the opium-eater's principal childhood impressions so that we may render more intelligible the musings which furnished the food for his everyday thoughts while he was at Oxford. The reader must not forget that this is an elderly man relating episodes from his childhood,* a man who, returning to that childhood, always reasons with subtlety; and finally, that this childhood, the basis of subsequent reveries, is reviewed and considered through the magic atmosphere of the dream, that is to say, through the dark reflections of opium.

VII. THE AFFLICTION OF CHILDHOOD*

He and his three sisters were very young when their father died, leaving their mother an abundant fortune, all the wealth of an English merchant. Luxury, well-being, and a splendid and elegant life are conditions very favorable to the development of the natural sensitivity of a child.

"Having no other playmates but three innocent little sisters, sleeping always among them and shut away forever in a beautiful and silent garden from all knowledge of poverty, oppression, or injustice, I had not suspected the true complexion of the world." More than once he rendered thanks to Providence for this incomparable privilege, not only for having been raised in rural seclusion, but "for having had my infant feelings shaped by the gentlest of sisters, and not *horrid pugilistic brothers*."* Indeed, men who have been brought up by women and among women little resemble other men, even assuming an equality in their temperaments or intellectual abilities. The nourishing cradle, the maternal caress, the gentle ways of sisters, especially older sisters, those diminutive mothers, so to speak, transform while kneading the masculine dough. The man who, from his earliest infancy, was bathed in the soft atmosphere of woman, with scented breast, hands, knees, and hair, all her supple and floating raiment,

> *Dulce balneum suavibus*
> *Unguentatum odoribus,**

thereby developed a mind constitutionally tender, delicate, a type of androgyny, without which the sharpest and most virile genius will remain, relative to the perfection of his art, an incomplete being. Finally, I will add that the early taste of the feminine world, *mundi muliebris,** of all that gauzelike drapery, shimmering·and perfumed, creates superior geniuses; and my highly intelligent female reader will, I trust, grant me this almost sensual form of expression, just as she will accept and understand the purity of my thought.

Jane died first. But for her little brother, her death was not yet something intelligible. Jane had only gone away; she would perhaps come back. A female servant, called upon to attend her during her illness, had treated her harshly two days before her death. The story was spread through the family, and from that moment on the boy could not ever bear to look the girl in the eye. When he saw her, he stared at the ground. This was not from anger, nor from feelings of revenge; what he felt was horror and foreboding, as the sensitivity contracted upon a first brutal glimpse of the truth, that he was in a world of evil, struggle, and strife.

The second wound to his infant heart was not so easily healed.

After an interval of a few happy years, his dear, noble Elizabeth, so precociously and elegantly intelligent, died too; so that when he summoned her sweet countenance in the darkness, he always imagined a tiara of light or a halo surrounding her ample brow. She was his elder by three years and had already shown a natural precedency of authority. The death of this beloved sister filled him with indescribable sorrow. On the day that followed her death, while her sweet remains were yet unviolated by scientific curiosity, he resolved to see his sister once more. "Grief, even in children, hates the light and shrinks from human eyes." There-fore, this supreme visit had to be kept secret and without witness. It was noon when he reached the door to her room, and nothing could he see at first but one large window, wide open, through which the hot midday sun was showering all of its splendors. "The weather was dry, the sky was cloudless, and the blue depths seemed to express a type of perfect infinity; and it was not possible for the eye to behold, or for the heart to conceive, any more pathetic symbol of life and the glory of life."

A great sorrow, an irreparable sorrow that strikes us at the year's most beautiful season carries, it is said, a more hellish and sinister character. As we have already remarked, I believe, in the analysis of the *Confessions*, death is more affecting during summer's pompous reign. "The reason lies in the antagonism between the tropical redundancy of life in summer and the dark sterilities of the grave. The summer we see; the grave we haunt with our thoughts. And when the two come into collision, each exalts the other into stronger relief." But for the child, who was later to become a scholar of powerful intellect and imagination, for the author of the *Confessions* and of the *Suspiria*, there was another reason that this antagonism had already strongly bound the images of summer and the idea of death—a reason which finds intimate relations between the landscape and the writings of the Scriptures. "Far more of our deepest thoughts and feelings pass to us through perplexed combinations of concrete objects, pass to us as involutes in compound experiences incapable of being disentangled, than ever reach us directly and in their own abstract shape." Thus the Bible, which the young nurse read to the children during the long dark evenings, greatly contributed toward uniting these two ideas in his imagination. The nurse, who knew the Orient, explained to them the differences in its climates, and all those differences that express themselves in the great varieties of summer. It was in an Oriental climate, in one of those lands that seems blessed by eternal summers, that a just man, man and yet not man, had suffered the *passion* of death in Palestine. The disciples plucking the ears of corn—that must obviously be summer; but, does not the very name of Palm Sunday also provide food for that dream? *Sunday*, the day of peace which masked another peace deeper than the heart of man can comprehend; *palms*, expressed the pomp of life and, as a product of nature, the pomp of summer. The great event of Jerusalem was at hand when Palm Sunday came; and the scene of that Sunday was near Jerusalem. Jerusalem, which had been considered as the navel, the center of the earth, as once had Delphi. But if not of the earth, Jerusalem may at least be the center of mortality. For it was there that Death had been trampled underfoot; it was there that Death had opened its most sinister crater.

So it was that on a magnificent summer's day, with the sun cruelly shining, he returned to the bedchamber of his sister, to look one last time upon her angelic face. He had heard it said in the house that none of her features had suffered any change. The forehead, indeed, was the same, but the marble lips and the stiffening hands were a terrible shock to him; and while he stood, a violent wind began to blow, "the most mournful," he said, "that he had ever heard." Many times thereafter, upon summer days, when the sun was at its hottest, he remarked the same wind arising and "uttering the same hollow, solemn, Memnonian,* but saintly swell." It is, he adds, the one sole audible symbol of eternity in this world. And three times in his life he heard the same sound in the same circumstances, namely, when standing between an open window and a dead body on a summer day.

All of a sudden, his eyes, filled with the golden fullness of life, contrasting the pomp and glory of the heavens outside with the frost which overspread his sister's face, beheld a srange vision. A vault seemed to open in the zenith of the far blue sky, a shaft which ran up forever. He rose in spirit on those azure billows; and the billows and his spirit seemed to pursue the throne of God, but that also ran before him and fled away continually. He fell asleep in that curious rapture, and when he recovered his self-possession, he found himself sitting again beside his sister's bed. The solitary child, overwhelmed by his first grief, flew toward God, that consummate solitary. Thus instinct, superior to all philosophy, allowed him to find in this celestial vision a fleeting instant of comfort. He then fancied he heard a step on the stairs. Trembling in fear lest anyone should detect him, for if anyone detected him, he would have been prevented from returning, he hastily kissed his sister's lips and stealthily crept from the room. The following day, the doctors came to examine her brain. He knew nothing of the nature of their visit, and some hours after they had gone, he crept again to the room, but the door was now locked and the key had been taken away. He was thus spared from seeing her dishonored by the ravages of science; he would keep a peaceful image of her, as immobile and pure as marble or ice.

And then came the funeral, which brought with it new agonies. He rode in a carriage with some indifferent gentlemen who talked of things that were foreign to his pain. The terrible harmonies of the organ and all of that Christian solemnity, too crushing for a child, and those religious promises that would raise his sister to heaven, were little consolation for him who had lost her on earth. At the church, he was told to hold a handkerchief to his eyes. Had he any need to affect a mournful countenance and pretend to cry, he who could barely stand on his feet? Light blazed in the stained glass windows where the apostles and the saints trampled their glory; and, in the days that followed, when he went to church, he saw through the wide window of uncolored glass, endless clouds of fleecy white transformed into curtains and white pillows, on which lay children, suffering, weeping, and dying. Slowly these beds went up to scale the heavens, ascending toward the God who had so loved his children. Later, a long while afterward, three passages from the funeral service, which he must certainly have heard but which he perhaps had not listened to or which had revived his pain through their too bitter consolations, were imprinted upon his memory, with their mysterious and deep meanings, speaking of deliverance, resurrection, and eternity, and became for him a frequent theme for thought. Soon after that time he tasted the consolations of solitude which, when acting with unresisted grief, ended in the paradoxical result of making out of grief itself a luxury; so all deep passions seek for solitude. The vast stillness of the countryside, the summers shot with gleaming light, the misty afternoons, held for him a dangerous attraction. He gazed into the sky and the fog, as if some comfort lay concealed in *them*. Pursuing something that could not be obtained, he beseeched the azure depths, searching them for one beloved image, a face that might, perhaps, have permission to reveal itself one more time. To my great regret, I must abridge for want of room the section that contains the lengthy narrative of the inescapable grief in which he was caught as in a labyrinth. All of nature is invoked here as each object becomes in turn *representative* of the central idea. From out of this grief will sometimes spring mournful, coquettish flowers, at once poignant and rich, the lovingly morbid tones of which are often transformed into witticisms. Does not even mourning serve here as fodder? And then, it is not solely sincerity of feeling that moves the spirit, for the critic will also find a new, unique pleasure, that of seeing throughout the narrative the passionate, delicate mysticism which generally flowers only in the gardens of the Roman Catholic Church. At last a time arrived when that morbid sensitivity, nourished exclusively on a memory, and that immoderate love of solitude, came to be transformed into a definite danger; one of those decisive, crucial times when the dispairing soul asks itself, "If those whom we love can come to us no more, what prevents us from joining them?"; times when the obsessed, fascinated imagination succumbs with pleasure to the "sublime attractions of the grave."* Fortunately, the time had come for work and necessary distractions. He was now forced to assume the harness of life and begin his classical studies.

Although the following pages are more lighthearted, we find the same sense of feminine tenderness, now applied to animals* —those interesting slaves of man—to cats, to dogs, to all those beings so easily shamed, oppressed, enchained. Indeed, does not the animal, by its unconscious joy and simplicity, in a way represent man's own infancy? Here, then, the gentleness of the young dreamer, while straying toward these new objects, stays faithful to his original character. He still loves, in their more or less perfect guises, weakness, innocence, and candor. Among the principal traits and characteristics assigned to him by destiny, we must also note an excessive delicacy of conscience which, combining with his extreme sensitivity, excessively enlarges the commonest deeds and extracts from the slightest mishaps, even imaginary ones, frightful terrors of a nature all too real. And thus we find this child, deprived of the object of his first and greatest affection, enamored of solitude, and without close friendship. And now the reader will clearly see how several of the phenomena that played out in the theater of his dreams had inevitably sprung from the trials of his earliest youth. The seeds of destiny had been sown; fed by opium, they bore a strange and abundant fruit. Childhood memories became, to use the author's metaphor, the natural coefficient of the opium. That preternatural faculty, which led him to idealize all things and endow them with supernatural proportions, long exercised and cultivated in solitude, and activated beyond measure by opium must, at Oxford, have produced grandiose and unwonted results, even among most young people of his generation.

The reader will recall the adventures of our hero in Wales, his sufferings in London, and the reconciliation with his guardians. We must now imagine him at Oxford, devoted to his studies and increasingly inclined to reverie, engendered by a substance he had first used to treat a toothache when he lived in London, and which proved a dangerous and powerful stimulant for his precociously dreamy faculties. From then on, his earlier life entered into this second life, to fashion a whole that was as personal as it was unusual. He occupied this new life that he might live again in the first. How many times did he revisit, during schooltime activities, the chamber where the body of his sister lay, that glorious summer light and the window of death, the road open to rapture through the vaults of the azure heavens; and then the priest in his white surplice standing by the side of an open grave, the coffin being lowered into the earth, and the *dust to dust*; finally the saints, the apostles, and the martyrs of the window, illuminated by the golden sunlight and creating a magnificient frame for those white beds, for those pretty cradles that went up, to the somber strains of the organ, to heaven! All of that he saw again, but saw it with variations, flourishes, in intense color or in a glorifying haze. He saw once again the whole universe of his childhood, but with the full poetic riches that a cultivated, subtle mind could add, a mind that was already accustomed to finding its greatest pleasures in solitude and memory.

VIII. OXFORD VISIONS*

The Palimpsest

"What is the human brain, if not an immense and natural palimpsest? Such a palimpsest is my brain; such is yours too, reader. Everlasting layers of ideas, images, and feelings have fallen upon your brain as softly as light. Each succession has seemed to bury all that went before. And yet, in reality, not one has perished." Nevertheless, between the palimpsest that carries, one superimposed over another, the Greek tragedy, the monkish legend, and the knightly romance, and the divine palimpsest created by God, which is our incommensurate memory, arises this difference, that there is something in the first of a fantastic, grotesque chaos, a collision between heterogeneous elements, whereas in the second the inevitability of temperament imposes a harmony among the most disparate elements. The fleeting accidents of a man's life may be incongruous, but the organizing principle remains undisturbed. All of the echoes of memory, awakened simultaneously, come forth as a concert which, whether pleasing or painful, is yet logical and free of dissonance.

It often happens that a person on the brink of death will see the theater of their life suddenly expanded and radiant within their brains. Time, then, becomes infinitely elastic, and a few seconds will hold the feelings and images of many years. And the true point for astonishment in this experience is not the simultaneity of arrangement under which the past events of life, though in fact successive, had formed this relevation, but the resurrection itself, and the possibility of resurrection for what had so long slept. What has passed from our memory is preserved in this true reflection, which we are compelled to *recognize* when it is arrayed before us as in a mirror; traces once impressed upon the memory are indestructible. By solemn circumstances, by death perhaps, by the intense stimulation of opium, all of the vast, complex palimpsest of the brain suddenly unfurls to reveal the superimposed strata of our past experience, mysteriously fixed in the phenomenon we call forgetfulness.

A melancholic, misanthropic man of genius, wishing to avenge himself on the injustice of his century, one day cast all of his manuscript works into the fire. And when he was criticized for this terrible holocaust inspired by hate, which indeed was the sacrifice of all his own hopes, he replied, "What could it matter? What is important is that these things were *created*; they were created, therefore they *are*." He endowed all created things with an indestructible character. How well and more obviously still that idea applies to all of our thoughts and actions, good or evil! And if there is something infinitely consoling in this belief, in the case when our mind turns toward that part of ourselves which we can view with complaisance, is there not also something infinitely terrible in it when the mind inevitably turns toward that part of ourselves which we cannot view without horror? In the spiritual as in the material world, nothing is lost. Just as every action, cast into the whirlwind of universal action, is in itself irrevocable and irreparable, an abstraction fashioned of its possible results, so all thought is likewise ineffaceable: the palimpsest of the memory is indestructible.

"Yes, reader, countless are the poems of grief or joy which have inscribed themselves succcessively upon the palimpsest of your brain; and, like the annual leaves of aboriginal forests, or the undissolving snows on the Himalayas, or light falling upon light, the endless strata have covered up each other in forgetfulness. But by the hour of death, but by fever, but by the searchings of opium, all these can revive in strength. They are not dead, but sleeping. The Grecian tragedy seemed to be displaced, but was *not* displaced, by the monkish legend; and the monkish legend had seemed to be displaced, but was *not* displaced, by the knightly romance. All wheels back into its earliest elementary stage. The bewildering romance, light tarnished with darkness, the semifabulous legend, these fade even of themselves as life advances. The romance has perished that the young man adored; the legend has gone that deluded the boy; but the deep tragedies of infancy, as when the child's hands were unlinked forever from his mother's neck, or his lips forever from his sister's kisses, live always concealed, beneath other legends of the palimpsest. Passion and illness have not powerful enough chemistry to burn away these immortal imprints."

Levana and Our Ladies of Sorrow

"Oftentimes at Oxford I saw Levana in my dreams. I knew her by her Roman symbols." But who is Levana? She was the Roman goddess that performed for the newborn infant the earliest office, so to speak, of ennobling kindness. "At the very moment of birth, just as the infant tasted for the first time the atmosphere of our troubled planet, it was laid on the ground. But immediately, lest so grand a creature should grovel there for more than one instant, either the paternal hand, as proxy for the goddess Levana, or some near kinsman, as proxy for the father, raised it upright, bade it look erect as the king of all this world, and presented its forehead to the stars, saying, perhaps, in his heart, 'Behold that which is greater than yourselves!' This symbolic act represented the function of Levana. And that mysterious lady, who never revealed her face (except to me in dreams), but always acted by delegation, had her name from the Latin verb *levare*, to raise aloft."

Hence it has arisen that some people have understood by

Levana the tutelary power that controls the education of the nursery. By the education of Levana is meant, not the poor machinery that moves by spelling books and grammars, "but by that mighty system of central forces hidden in the deep bosom of human life, which by passion, by strife, by temptation, by the energies of resistance, works forever upon children." Levana ennobles the human beings she watches over, but by cruel means. She is harsh and severe, that good nurse, and among the ministries by which she works to perfect the human creature, that which she reverences above all is the agency of grief. Three goddesses serve her, whom she employs in her mysterious designs. As the *Graces* are three, the *Parcae* are three, and the *Furies* are three, so three are the goddesses of sorrow. They are *Our Ladies of Sorrow.*

"Them I saw often conversing with Levana, and sometimes about myself. Do they talk, then? Oh, no! Mighty phantoms like these disdain the infirmities of language. They may utter voices through the organs of man when they dwell in human hearts, but amongst themselves there is no voice nor sound; eternal silence reigns in their kingdoms. ... The eldest of the three is named *Mater Lachrymarum*, Our Lady of Tears. She it is that night and day raves and moans, calling for vanished faces. She stood in Rama, where a voice was heard of lamentation—Rachel weeping for her children, and refusing to be comforted. She it was who stood in Bethlehem on the night when Herod's sword swept its nurseries of Innocents... Her eyes are sweet and subtle, wild and sleepy, by turns, oftentimes rising to the clouds, oftentimes challenging the heavens. She wears a diadem round her head. And I knew by childish memories that she could go abroad upon the winds, when she heard the sobbing of litanies or the thundering of organs, and when she beheld the mustering of summer clouds. This sister, the eldest, it is that carries keys more than papal at her girdle, which open every cottage and every palace. She, to my knowledge, sat all last summer by the bedside of the blind beggar, him that so often and so gladly I talked with, whose pious daughter, eight years old, with the sunny countenance, resisted the temptations of play and village mirth to travel all day long on dusty roads with her afflicted father. For this did God send her a great reward. In the springtime of the year, and while yet in her own spring, he recalled her to himself. But her blind father mourns forever over her; still he dreams at midnight that the little guiding hand is locked within his own; and still he wakens to a darkness that is now within a second and a deeper darkness. . . . By the power of the keys it is that Our Lady of Tears glides, a ghostly intruder, into the chambers of sleepless men, sleepless women, sleepless children, from the Ganges to the Nile, from the Nile to the Mississippi. And her, because she is the firstborn of her house, and has the vastest empire, let us honor with the title of Madonna.

"The second sister is called *Mater Suspiriorum*—Our Lady of Sighs. She never scales the clouds, nor walks abroad upon the winds. She wears no diadem. And her eyes, if they were ever seen, would be neither sweet nor subtle; no man could read their story. They would be found filled with perishing dreams and with wrecks of forgotten delirium. But she raises not her eyes. Her head, on which sits a dilapidated turban, drops forever, forever fastens on the dust. She weeps not. She groans not. But she sighs inaudibly at intervals. Her sister, Madonna, is oftentimes stormy and frantic, raging in the highest against heaven, and demanding back her darlings. But Our Lady of Sighs never clamors, never defies, dreams not of rebellious aspirations. She is humble to abjectness. Hers is the meekness that belongs to the hopeless. Murmur she may, but it is to herself in the twilight. Mutter she does at times, but it is in solitary places that are desolate as she is desolate, in ruined cities, and when the sun has gone down to his rest. This sister is the visitor of the pariah. . . of the woman sitting in the darkness, without love to shelter her head, without hope to illuminate her solitude, of every captive in his prison; all who are betrayed and all who are rejected; outcasts of traditional law and children of hereditary disgrace: all these walk with Our Lady of Sighs. She also carries a key, but she needs it little. For her kingdom is chiefly amongst the tents of Shem and the houseless vagrant of every clime. Yet in the very highest walks of man she finds chapels of her own; and even in glorious England there are some that, to the world, carry their heads as proudly as the reindeer, who yet secretly have received her mark upon their foreheads.

"But the third sister, who is also the youngest—! Hush, whisper whilst we talk of her! Her kingdom is not large, or else no flesh should live, but within that kingdom all power is hers. . . . Through the treble veil of crepe which she wears, the fierce light of a blazing misery, that rests not for matins or for vespers, for noon of day or noon of night, for ebbing or for flowing tide, may be read from the very ground. She is the defier of God. She is also the mother of lunacies, and the suggestress of suicides. . . . Madonna moves with uncertain steps, fast or slow, but still with tragic grace. Our Lady of Sighs creeps timidly and stealthily. But this youngest sister moves with incalculable motions, bounding, and with tiger's leaps. She carries no key; for, though coming rarely amongst men, she storms all doors at which she is permitted to enter at all. And her name is *Mater Tenebrarum*—Our Lady of Darkness.

"These were the *Eumenides*, or Gracious Ladies (so called by antiquity in shuddering propitiation), of my Oxford dreams. Madonna spoke. She spoke by her mysterious hand. Touching my head, she beckoned to Our Lady of Sighs. And what she spoke, translated out of the signs which (except in dreams) no man reads, was this: 'Lo! here is he, whom in childhood I dedicated to my altars. This is he that once I made my darling.

Him I led astray, him I beguiled, and from heaven I stole away his young heart to mine. Through me did he become idolatrous; and through me it was, by languishing desires, that he worshiped the worm and prayed to the wormy grave. Holy was the grave to him; lovely was its darkness; saintly its corruption. Him, this young idolator, I have seasoned for thee, dear gentle Sister of Sighs! Do thou take him now to thy heart and season him for our dreadful sister. And thou,'—turning to the *Mater Tenebrarum*, she said—'wicked sister, that temptest and hatest, do thou take him from her. See that thy scepter lies heavy on his head. Suffer not woman and her tenderness to sit near him in his darkness. Banish the frailties of hope, wither the relenting of love, scorch the fountain of tears, curse him as only thou canst curse. So shall he be accomplished in the furnace, so shall he see the things that ought not to be seen, sights that are abominable and secrets that are unutterable. So shall he read elder truths, sad truths, grand truths, fearful truths. So shall he rise again before he dies, and so shall our commission be accomplished which from God we had—to plague his heart until we had unfolded the capacities of his spirit.'"

The Specter of the Brocken*

On a beautiful Whitsunday,* let us climb the Brocken. Dazzling cloudless dawn! Yet April sometimes frets the renewed season with showers and capricious storms. We gain the mountain's summit; on such a morning, we shall have one chance the more for seeing the famous Specter of the Brocken. This specter has lived so long among pagan sorcerers, he has witnessed so many dark idolatries, that his heart may have been corrupted and his faith shaken. Make first the sign of the cross, as a test, and observe whether he consents to repeat it. He does repeat it, but these driving April showers perplex the images, and that, perhaps, it is which gives him the air of one who acts reluctantly or evasively. Now we will try him again, "gather one of these anemones which were once called the sorcerer's flower,* and which once perhaps glorified this horrible worship of fear. Lay it upon the stone that imitates the form of a pagan altar; then, bending your knee, and raising your right hand, say, 'Father, which art in Heaven.... I, thy servant, and this dark phantom, whom for one hour on this thy Pentecost I make my servant, render these united worships upon this, thy recovered temple!' Lo! The apparition plucks an anemone and places it on the altar; he also bends his knee; he also raises his right hand to God. Dumb he is, but sometimes the dumb serve God acceptably."

Yet still it occurs to you that the specter, having so long been accustomed to a blind devotion, may pledge devotion to all religions, and that his natural servility renders his homage insignificant. Let us then seek another means to try the nature of this singular being. If, then, once in childhood you suffered an affliction that was ineffable; if once, you suffered an incurable despair—in that case, after the example of Judea (on the Roman coins), sitting under her palm tree to weep, but sitting with her head veiled, do you also weep, in commemoration of that great woe. The apparition of the Brocken has already veiled *his* head, as if he had a human heart and as if he wished to express by a silent symbol the memory of a sorrow that was unutterable by words. "This trial is decisive. You are now satisfied that the apparition is but a reflex of yourself; and, in uttering your secret feelings to *him*, you make this phantom the dark symbolic mirror for reflection to the daylight what else must be hidden forever."

Such a relation does the Dark Interpreter, whom the reader will know as an intruder into the opium-eater's dreams, bear to his own mind. But as the apparition of the Brocken sometimes is disturbed by storms or by driving showers, in like manner the Mysterious Interpreter at times mingles with alien natures.

"What he says, generally, is but that which I have said in daylight, and in meditation deep enough to inscribe itself on my heart. But sometimes, as his face alters, his words alter; and they do not always seem such as I have used or _could_ use. No man can account for all things that occur in dreams. Generally I believe this: that he is a faithful representative of myself, but he also is at times subject to the action of the good _Phantasus_, who rules in dreams." One might say that he bears the office of a chorus in a Greek tragedy. But the leading function of both must be supposed this: not to tell you anything new, that was done by the actors in the drama; but to recall you to your own thoughts, hidden for the moment or imperfectly developed, and to place before you such commentaries, prophetic or looking back, pointing to the moral or deciphering the mystery, justifying Providence, or mitigating the fierceness of anguish, as would have occurred to your own meditative heart, had only time been allowed for its motions.

Savannah-La-Mar

To that melancholic gallery of paintings, vast and affecting allegories of sadness, in which I found (I know not whether the reader, seeing them only in this abridged form, will experience the same sensation) a charm as musical as it is picturesque, I shall add another section, which can be considered as the finale to a great symphony.

"God smote Savannah-la-Mar, and in one night, by earthquake, removed her, with all her towers standing and population sleeping, from the steadfast foundations of the shore to the coral floors of ocean. And God said, 'Pompeii did I bury and conceal from men through seventeen centuries; this city I will bury, but not conceal. She shall be a monument to men of my mysterious anger, set in azure light through generations to come, for I will enshrine her in a crystal dome of my tropic seas.' And oftentimes in glassy calms, through the translucid atmosphere of water, mariners from every clime look down into her courts and terraces, count her gates, and number the spires of her churches. Ample cemetery, she fascinates the eye with a revelation as of human life still subsisting in submarine asylums sacred from the storms that torment our atmosphere." Oftentimes in dreams did he and the Dark Interpreter visit the inviolate solitude of Savannah-la-Mar. Together they looked into the belfries, where the pendulous bells were waiting in vain for the summons which should awaken their marriage peals; together they touched the organ keys that sang no jubilates for the ear of heaven, that sang no requiems for the ear of human sorrow; together they searched the silent nurseries where the children were all asleep, and had been asleep through five generations.

"'They are waiting for the heavenly dawn,' whispered the Interpreter to himself, 'and when that comes, the bells and the organs will utter a jubilate repeated by the echoes of Paradise.' Then, turning to me, he said, 'This is sad, this is piteous, but less would not have sufficed for the purposes of God. Look here.... The time which *is* contracts into a mathematic point, and even that point perishes a thousand times before we can utter its birth. All is finite in the present, and even that finite is infinite in its velocity of flight toward death. But in God there is nothing finite; but in God there is nothing transitory; but in God there can be nothing that tends to death. Therefore it follows that for God there can be no present. The future is the present of God, and to the future it is that he sacrifices the human present. Therefore it is that he works by earthquake. Therefore it is that he works by grief. Oh, deep is the plowing of the earthquake! Oh, deep'—and his voice swelled like a Sanctus rising from the choir of a cathedral—'Oh, deep is the plowing of grief! But oftentimes less would not suffice for the agriculture of God. Upon a night of earthquake he builds a thousand years of pleasant habitations for man. Upon the sorrow of an infant he raises oftentimes from human intellects glorious vintages that could not else have been. Less than these fierce plowshares would not have stirred the stubborn soil. The one is needed for earth, our planet, for earth itself as the dwelling place of man; but the other is needed yet oftener for God's mightiest instrument; yes—' and he looked solemnly at myself—'is needed for the mysterious children of the earth!'"

IX. CONCLUSION

Despite their generally symbolic character, these long reveries and poetic representations better *illustrate*, for the discerning reader, the moral character of our author than would the later anecdotes or autobiograhical sketches. In the final section of the *Suspiria*, he revisits with apparent pleasure the years that are already so distant and, here as elsewhere, what is truly precious is not the event but the commentary, commentary that is often dark, bitter, and desolate. Solitary thought aspires to fly far above the earth and far above the theater of human strife with great wing-beats toward heaven. Here is the monologue of a soul that was always too easily wounded; here, as in the sections already analyzed, his thought is the caduceus of which he has so pleasantly spoken with the candor of a vagabond who knows his own mind. The subject has no more value than that of a simple staff, bare and dry, but the ribbons, the garlands, the flowers may, as they madly intertwine, render a richness precious to the eyes. De Quincey's thought is not only sinuous; his word is not strong enough: his thought naturally spirals. Indeed, these commentaries and reflections are too lengthy to analyze, and I must remember that the goal of this work was to show, by example, the effects of opium on a meditative mind inclined to reverie. This goal, I believe, has been accomplished.

I will content myself with saying that the solitary thinker revisits with some satisfaction the precocious sensitivity which for him was the source of so many horrors and so many pleasures; he revisits his immense love for liberty and the shock of the events that inspired responsibility. "The horror of life mixed itself already in earliest youth with the heavenly sweetness of life." There is, in these last pages of the *Suspiria*, something funereal, corrosive, aspiring to things other than of this earth. Regarding his youthful adventures, he still has the good spirits and grace to jest in the midst of his own misery. But what is most prophetic and what is most striking are the lyrical explosions of incurable melancholy. For example, apropos of those beings who constrain our liberty, hurt our feelings, and violate the most legitimate rights of our youth, he cries, "Oh, wherefore is it that those who presume to call themselves the 'friends' of this man or that woman are so often those, above all others, whom in the hour of death that man or woman is most likely to salute with this valediction: 'Would God I had never seen your face'?" Or as when he cynically utters this avowal which, I confess, has for me the same candor, and an almost fraternal charm: "Generally speaking, the few people whom I have disliked in this world were flourishing people, of good repute. Whereas the knaves whom I have known, one and all, and by no means few, I think of with pleasure and kindness." We note, in passing, that this graceful reflection also applies to the disreputable attorney whose apartments he tenanted in London. Or as when he states that, if life could magically throw open its long suites of chambers from some station *beforehand*—if our eyes young again, could look by anticipation along its vast corridors, and aside into the recesses opening upon them, halls of future tragedies or chambers of retribution—what a recoil we and our friends should suffer of horror in our estimate of life! After having painted a picture of well-being, splendor, and domestic purity, with grace and a wealth of inimitable colors, of beauty and goodness framed in luxury, he successively shows us the gracious heroines of the family, from mother to daughter, each, in her turn, under the heavy cloud of affliction; and he concludes by saying: "Death we can face: but knowing, as some of us do, what is human life, which of us is it that without shuddering could (if consciously we were summoned) face the hour of birth?"

I find a note at the bottom of one page which, in light of De Quincey's recent death, takes on a lugubrious significance.* According to the author's intention, the *Suspiria de Profundis* was to have been curiously expanded. He terminated the book as at a natural pause, with the legend of Our Ladies of Sorrow, which, he tells us, prefigures the course of his future works. Thus, as the first section (the death of Elizabeth and her brother's sorrow) logically belongs to the Madonna, or Our Lady of Tears, so a new part, *The Pariah Worlds*, was to belong to Our Lady of Sighs; and finally, Our Lady of Darkness was to belong to *The Kingdom of Darkness*. But Death menaces all of our plans and grants us no choice, lets us dream of happiness and says neither no nor yes; Death with flying haste springs from ambush to sweep away, with a single wing beat, all of our plans, our dreams, and the ideal structures in which we shelter the thoughts of glory of our last days!

The Texts

1. *Du vin et du hachish: Le Messager de l'Assemblée*, 7, 8, 11, and 12 March 1851.
2. *Les Paradis artificiels.* Three versions exist, the last of which was posthumous.
   a. "De L'Idéal artificiel—*Le Haschisch*" (the text of "Le Poème du Haschisch"), *La Revue contemporaine*, 30 September 1858. "Enchantements et tortures d'un mangeur d'opium" (the text of "Un Mangeur d'opium") appeared in the same review, 15 and 31 January 1860.
   b. Baudelaire reworked the two *Revue contemporaine* articles and combined them for publication as a separate volume. *Les Paradis artificiels, opium et haschisch* was published by Poulet-Malassis et de Broise in 1860.
   c. *Oeuvres complètes de Charles Baudelaire*, Michel Lévy Frères, Paris, 1869. The text of this edition is essentially that of the 1860 volume, with a few variants. It is in this collection that the 1851 article "Du Vin et du hachish" first appeared together with *Les Paradis artificiels*.

Théophile Gautier
1. "La Pipe d'opium." *La Presse*, 27 September 1838.
2. "Le Hachich." *La Presse*, 10 July 1843.
3. "Le Club des hachichins." *Revue des deux mondes*, 1 February 1846.
4. "Charles Baudelaire." *L'Univers Illustré*, 7, 14, 21, 28 March and 4, 11, 18 April 1868

Note: The orthography of "hashish" has been normalized in the English text. The numerous variant spellings of the word in French have been retained in the citations of titles.

Select Bibliography

I. STANDARD EDITIONS

BAUDELAIRE.

Oeuvres complètes, ed. Y. G. Le Dantec et C. Pichois, 2 vols., Bibliothèque de la Pléiade, Paris, 1975. The fullest and only complete edition of Baudelaire's writings.

Correspondance, ed. C. Pichois et J. Ziegler, 2 vols., Bibliothèque de la Pléiade, Paris, 1951.

DE QUINCEY.

The Collected Writings of Thomas De Quincey, 14 vols., A. & C. Black, Edinburgh, 1889–90. This edition, reviewed and revised by the author, has been reprinted several times.

De Quincey's Writings, 23 vols. Ticknor, Reed and Fields, Boston, 1850–59.

II. CRITICAL EDITIONS AND NINETEENTH-CENTURY SOURCES

Asselineau, C. *Baudelaire, sa vie et son oeuvre*. Paris, 1869.

Bandy, W. T., and J. Mouquet. *Baudelaire Judged by His Contemporaries (1845–1867)*. Publications of the Institute of French Studies, Inc., Columbia University, New York, 1933.

Banville, Th. de. *Mes Souvenirs*. Paris, 1931.

Clapton, G. T. *Baudelaire et De Quincey*. Société d'Edition "Les Belles Lettres." Paris, 1931.

Gautier, Th. *Portraits contemporains*. Paris, 1874.

Pichois, C., and J. Dagens, eds. *Lettres à Charles Baudelaire.*
  Neuchâtel, 1973.
Ruff, M. *Baudelaire, l'homme et l'oeuvre.* Paris, 1957.
Sartre, J.-P. *Baudelaire.* Paris, 1947.
Starkie, E. *Baudelaire.* London, 1957.
Verlaine, P. *Oeuvres en Prose complètes,* ed. Jacques Borel. Paris,
  1972.

Notes

On Wine and Hashish

3　Brillat-Savarin: Anthelme Brillat-Savarin (1755–1826), French gastronome, author of *La Physiologie du goût* (1825). These barbs directed against the fashionable gastronome of the day were perhaps provoked by his claim that "water is the only drink truly capable of quenching the thirst."

3　inhabitant of the moon: A recollection of Swedenborg's *Earths in the Universe* (1758), in which the spirit inhabitants of the planets and the moon wander throughout the universe in a quest for knowledge.

4　Lavater: Johann Caspar Lavater (1741–1801), Swiss philosopher, religious poet, and theologian.

4　Hoffmann: Ernest Theodor Hoffmann (1776–1822). The *Kreisleriana* was included in Hoffmann's first book, a collection of fantastic stories and essays entitled *Fantasiestücke in Callots Manier* (4 vols., 1814–15). In his *Salon* of 1846, Baudelaire quotes from the *Kreisleriana:* "It is not only in my dreams and in the reverie that precedes slumber, but also in my waking thoughts that I hear music, that I find an analogy, an intimate union of colors, sounds, and scents. All of these elements unite as if they had sprung from the same flash of light, to join together in a marvellous concert."

4　*Le Moyen de parvenir:* A quotation from Bérolade de Verville, as published by Bibliophile Jacob, Charles Gosselin, 1841. The lines read: "Il y en a qui voient le jour par le cul, comme vous diriez les chaudronniers, et ceux et celles qui travaillent de l'aiguille, et les buveurs, qui voient le cul et le montrent aux autres."

6　the voice of wine: See "L'Ame du vin" in *Les Fleurs du mal* for a similar tribute to wine. Themes from the five-poem cycle "Le Vin" in *Les Fleurs du mal* are seen in this prose-poem passage.

7　by the somber red glow of street lamps: See "Le Vin des chiffoniers" in *Les Fleurs du mal*.

8　Pactolus: A river of ancient Lydia whose waters ran with gold.

9   Drölling: Martin Drölling (1752–1827), genre painter. His *Intérieur de Cuisine* hangs in the Louvre.

12   Frédérick and Kean: Frédérick Lemaître (1800–1876), French actor, and Edmund Kean (1787–1833), British tragic actor.

19   Sound holds color: See Baudelaire's sonnet "Correspondances" in *Les Fleurs du mal*. Théophile Gautier, in his article "Le Hachich," writes that the drug brings to his ear a magnifying power, so that he hears sound in colors: "Green, blue, red, and yellow sounds wash over me in waves, each perfectly distinct."

20   *La Peau de Chagrin*: Balzac's novel was published in 1831.

25   Barbereau: Auguste Barbereau (1799–1879), French musician. As a friend of Boissard, he was frequently invited to parties at the Hôtel Pimodan.

25   The doctor: The allusion is to Dr. Moreau of Tours, author of *Du Hachisch et de l'aliénation mentale* (Paris, 1845).

Artificial Paradises

To J.G.F.

29   To J.G.F.: Baudelaire's dedication first appeared affixed to the edition of 1860. He also dedicated "L'Héautontimorouménos" (The Self-Tormentor) in the second edition of *Les Fleurs du mal* to the same woman, whose identity has never been discovered.

30   a lone, melancholy man who wanders: In the *Confessions*, De Quincey writes, "I walked in London, a solitary and contemplative man." The "lone man who wanders" appears again in "Les Foules" in *Le Spleen de Paris*. The poet may also be alluding to Rousseau's *Confessions et les Rêveries du promeneur solitaire*.

The Poem of Hashish

I. A Taste for the Infinite

31   Hoffmann: In "On Wine and Hashish," Baudelaire speaks of Hoffmann at greater length. The reader will notice, in "The Poem of Hashish," several passages that were taken from the "hashish" section of the 1851 study.

32   magic mirror: In "Le Mauvais vitrier," in *Le Spleen de Paris*,

Baudelaire writes, "What, have you no colored glass, pink, red, or blue, magic windows, windows of paradise?"

32   the author of *Lazare:* Auguste Barbier (1805–1882), French poet. A short study, in which Baudelaire praises Barbier's work, appeared in *La Revue fantasiste*, 15 July 1861.

33   the Spirit of Evil: Throughout "The Poem of Hashish," Baudelaire insists on the intervention of a supernatural agency that acts independently on the individual. The influence of Evil Spirits does not figure in the poet's earlier study of hashish. Flaubert objected to these remarks, in which he saw evidence of "a leavening of Catholicism."

34   which has not yet been translated into French in its entirety: An allusion to the 1828 adaptation of the *Confessions*, published as *L'Anglais Mangeur d'opium*. The book bore only the initials A.D.M., but was known to be the work of Alfred de Musset.

II. What Is Hashish?

34   the Old Man of the Mountain: It is worth noting that De Quincey writes on the same subject in his article "On Murder Considered as One of the Fine Arts" (1827): "The name 'Old Man of the Mountains' does not designate any individual person, but was the title—in Arabic *Sheikh-al-jebal*, "Prince of the Mountain"—of a series of chiefs who presided from 1090 to 1258 over a community or military order of fanatical Mohammedan sectaries, called *The Assassins,* distributed through Persia and Syria, but with certain mountain ranges for their headquarters. But, though there is no doubt that the words *assassin* and *assassination,* as terms for secret murder, and especially for secret murder by stabbing, are a recollection of the reputed habits of this old Persian and Syrian community, the original etymology of the word *Assassins* itself, as the name of the community, is not so certain. Skeat sets it down as simply the Arabic *hashishin,* "hashish-drinkers," from the fact or on the supposition that the agents of the Old Man of the Mountains, when they were detached on their murderous errands, went forth nerved for the task by the intoxication of *hashish,* or Indian hemp."

Gautier, in "Le Hachich," writes: "On this hashish the Old Man of the Mountains fed his subjects before sending them forth on their murderous missions. Hence the word *assassin* is derived from *hashishin*—hashish eater."

35   Mr. von Hammer: Josef von Hammer (1774–1856), Austrian scholar, author of *Geschichte der Assassinen* (1818). From his publisher Baudelaire obtained the French translation of this book, published in 1833 as *L'Histoire des assassins*.

35   Mr. Silvestre de Sacy: Antoine-Issac Silvestre de Sacy (1758–1838), author of "L'Histoire de la dynastie des assassins" (1818). He read his lecture "Mémoire sur la dynastie des assassins et sur l'origine de leur nom" to the Academy in 1809.

38   In the *Revue contemporaine* text (30 September 1858), an asterisk following the last word of the chapter refers the reader to this note: "To insure greater accuracy, I have had these documents reviewed by the current director of the Dorvault pharmacy, which has, for several years, stocked various preparations of hashish made from Bengalese hemp." Poulet-Malassis had suggested that the note be expanded for the 1860 edition; in exchange, Dorvault was to have carried the book in his shop. Baudelaire at length decided to omit the note. "Now I'm not joking," he told his publisher, "the pharmaceutical note at the work's close terrifies me. Consider well; one ill-wisher at some miserable newspaper would be enough to cause us great embarrassment."

Baudelaire relied on Dorvault, author of *L'Officine ou Répertoire général de pharmacie pratique,* for most of his botanical information. Dorvault's book, first published in 1844, was revised and expanded in 1847, 1850, and 1855. Baudelaire was also greatly indebted to Brierre de Boissmont's study, *Des Hallucinations* (1845).

III. The Seraphim Theater

38   Seraphim Theater: The Théâtre de Séraphin, boulevard Montmartre, staged marionette and shadow plays for children.

39   he wished to be an angel and he has become a beast: From Pascal, who wrote, "L'homme n'est ni ange ni bête; et le malheur veut que qui veut faire l'ange fait la bête."

50   *Esther:* One of Racine's biblical tragedies (1689). Baudelaire here refers to act 3, scene 5, in which Aman drops on one knee to the queen to ask her pardon.

50   Meissonier: Jean Louis Ernest Meissonier (1815–1891), French painter, whose work Baudelaire praised in his articles of art criticism.

54   The boudoir: The boudoir described here is that of the Hôtel Pimodan.

55   warbled with metal throats: See "L'Horlage" in *Les Fleurs du mal.*

IV. God-Made Man

59   Edgar Poe: Baudelaire here quotes from Poe's "Ligeia," "Berenice," and "A Tale of the Ragged Mountains." Baudelaire translated all three tales: "Ligeia," *Le Pays,* 3 and 4 February 1855; "Bérénice," *L'Illustration,* 17 April 1852; and "Les Souvenirs de M. Auguste Bedloe" (A Tale of the Ragged Mountains), *L'Illustration,* 11 December 1852.

63   Fourier: Charles Fourier (1772–1837), French social critic and philosopher. His theories for transforming society were based on cosmological beliefs and "analogical" methods. His three major works are *Théorie des quatre mouvements et des destinées générales* (1808); *Théorie de l'unité universelle* (1822); and *Le Nouveau Monde industriel et sociétaire* (1829).

63   Swedenborg: Emmanuel Swedenborg (1688–1772), Swedish theologian and mystic. According to his theory of "correspondences," the physical world is purely symbolical of the spiritual realm. For more information on this topic, I refer the reader to the following English translations of his works: *The Principia; or, The First Principles of Natural Things, Being New Attempts Toward a Philosophical Explanation of the Elementary World* (London, 1846); *The Infinite and the Final Cause of Creation, Also the Intercourse Between the Soul and the Body* (London, 1908); *A Philosopher's Note Book: Excerpts From Philosophical Writers and From the Sacred Scriptures on a Variety of Philosophical Subjects, Together With Some Reflections, and Sundry Notes and Memoranda by Emmanuel Swedenborg* (Philadelphia, 1931).

66   Pliny: Pliny the Elder (A.D. 23–79), Roman naturalist, author of *Natural History.*

66   lingam: From the Sanskrit *linga,* symbol of the Indian god Siva.

69   Jean-Jacques: Jean-Jacques Rousseau (1712–1778), Swiss philoso-

pher, author of *La Nouvelle Héloïse* (1761), *Le Contrat social* (1762), and *Emile* (1762). He believed that man, born good, is corrupted by society and must therefore strive to regain his original virtue: "L'homme naît bon, la société le corrompt." On this subject Baudelaire once said, "The naturally good man would be a monster, that is to say, a *God*" (letter to Alphonse Toussenel, 21 January 1856).

V. Moral

72   Melmoth: Hero of *Melmoth the Wanderer* (1820) by Charles Maturin.

72   at a party: A meeting of the Club des Hachichins at the Hôtel Pimodan. Gautier, who also attended, adds: "On handing back the spoonful of dawamesk, Balzac stated that the hashish could have no effective power over a mind as strong as his own."

72   Louis Lambert: In Balzac's autobiographical novel *Louis Lambert* (1832–33), the author's alter ego writes a *Traité de la volonté*, in which he examines the physical properties of the power of will.

73   indispensable pain: In "Benediction" (*Les Fleurs du mal*), Baudelaire writes: "Soyez béni, mon Dieu qui donnez la sourfrance / Comme un divin remède a nos impuretés."

75   Mantegna: Andrea Mantegna (1431–1506), Italian painter.

75   Francheville: Pierre de Francheville (c. 1548–c. 1615), French sculptor, also known by his Italian name, Pietro Francavilla. His works can be seen at the Louvre.

75   Goltzius: Hendrik Goltzius (1558–1616), Dutch engraver. Baudelaire modeled two poems in *Les Fleurs du mal* after Goltzius prints: "L'Amour et le crâne" after "Quis evadet?" and "Les Plaintes d'un Icare" after "Icarus."

AN OPIUM-EATER

I. Rhetorical Precautions

77   Oh! just, subtle, and mighty opium!: Baudelaire transferred this passage, taken from the close of "The Pleasures of Opium," to the

opening of his translation. He also omits the quotation marks that set off most of De Quincey's citations. De Quincey adapted the lines from Sir Walter Raleigh's *History of the World:* "O eloquent, just, and mighty Death!" Other references here include "the pangs that tempt the spirit to rebel" from William Wordsworth, "The White Doe of Rylstone," Dedication, 36; "Wrongs undressed, and insults unavenged," from Wordsworth, "The Excursion," iii, 374; and "from the anarchy of dreaming sleep," from Wordsworth, *The Excursion,* iv, 87.

78   reprehensible ends: De Quincey wrote: "with a view toward suicide."

79   touched with pensiveness: From "The Affliction of Childhood," *Suspiria de Profundis.*

79   caduceus: The source of these lines is a passage from the "Introductory Notice" to the *Suspiria de Profundis:* "I tell my critic that the whole course of this narrative resembles, and was meant to resemble, a *caduceus* wreathed about with meandering ornaments, or the shaft of a tree's stem hung round and surmounted with some vagrant parasitical plant. The mere medical subject of the opium answers to the dry withered pole, which shoots all the rings of the flowering plants, and seems to do so by some dexterity of its own; whereas, in fact, the plant and its tendrils have curled round the sullen cylinder by mere luxuriance of *theirs*...so, also, the ugly pole—hop pole, vine pole, espalier, no matter what—is there only for support. Not the flowers are for the pole, but the pole is for the flowers. Upon the same analogy view me, as one (in the words of a true and most impassioned poet) "viridantem floribus hastas"— making verdant, and gay with the life of flowers, murderous spears and halberts—things that express death in their origin (being made from dead substances that once had lived in forests), things that express ruin in their use. The true object in my 'Opium Confessions' is not the naked physiological theme—on the contrary, *that* is the ugly pole, the murderous spear, the halbert—but those wandering musical variations upon the theme—those parasitical thoughts, feelings, digressions, which climb up with bells and blossoms round about the arid stock; ramble away from it at times with perhaps too

rank a luxuriance; but at the same time, by the eternal interest attached to the *subjects* of these digressions, no matter what were the execution, spread a glory over incidents that for themselves would be—less than nothing." Baudelaire returns to the caduceus in the book's final chapter, "Conclusion." See also "Le Thyrse" in *Le Spleen de Paris.*

II. Preliminary Confessions

81   seven years old: De Quincey's narrative opens in the year 1792.

81   archididascalus: "As the professor loved to be called" (De Quincey).

82   feminine style: Baudelaire refers on several occasions to De Quincey's "feminine" style.

83   the ancient towers of ____: The college church of Manchester (revised edition of 1856).

84   the lady of the ten guineas: De Quincey later revealed that Lady Carbery had sent him the ten guineas; as to the lady of the portrait, he says only "the housekeeper was in the habit of telling me that the lady had 'lived' (meaning, perhaps, had been 'born') two centuries ago." He adds that the portrait was said to be a copy of a Van Dyke and that the "unknown lady" was a benefactress of the school.

85   With Atlantean shoulders... Monarchies: Milton, *Paradise Lost,* ii, 306–7.

86   with Providence my guide: Adapted from Milton, *Paradise Lost,* xii, 647.

86   a favorite English poet: William Wordsworth, as identified in the 1856 edition.

86   an accident: In order to arrange for financial support, De Quincey first visited his mother's home in Chester.

86   B____: Bangor (1856).

86   the Head: The common colloquial name for Holyhead.

88   Llan-y-styndw: De Quincey added, "or some such name." The correct form is Llanystumdwy.

88   keepsakes: At this point in the narrative of the 1856 edition, De Quincey speaks of keepsakes and "never-ending forget-me-nots."

88   The author fails to tell us: In the 1856 edition, De Quincey tells us that his Welsh friends had furnished him with the money he needed

to travel. After reaching Shrewsbury on foot, he proceeded to London by the Holyhead Mail.

89 hunger-bitten: In "The Prelude," ix, 510–11, Wordsworth writes, "We chanced one day to meet a hunger-bitten girl."

90 human nature explodes: These comments on moral suffering are introduced by Baudelaire.

92 laid down his conscience: In his article "Coleridge and Opium-Eating" (*Blackwood's*, 1845), De Quincey writes: "Coleridge charged the archdeacon repeatedly with his own joke, as if it had been a serious saying—viz., 'that he could not afford to keep a conscience'; such luxuries, like a carriage, for instance, being obviously beyond the finances of poor men."

93 shocking: This passage is entirely Baudelaire's, beginning with his comments on English literature and ending with the reference to Goethe's Marguerite.

94 the Bedouin of civilization: This paragraph is entirely Baudelaire's.

96 the Earl of ___: The Earl of Altamont (1856). De Quincey's boyhood friend Lord Westport, later the Earl of Altamont.

96 the Marquis of ___. The Marquis of Sligo (1856).

97 Lord ___: Lord Desart, cousin of Lord Westport (1856).

101 to ___: Grasmere (1856).

III. The Pleasures of Opium

102 pharmakon nepenthes: An anodyne. In the *Confessions* and in the *Revue contemporaine* text, φαρμακον νήπενθες. Cf. "Le Léthé" in *Les Fleurs du mal*.

102 *L'Allegro... Il Penseroso*: Two early poems of Milton's.

104 the late Duke of ___: The late Duke of Norfolk (1856).

105 Grassini: Josephine Grassini (1773–1850), Italian contralto.

107 like the bee: De Quincey elaborates in the 1856 edition: "In the large capacious chimneys of the rustic cottages throughout the Lake district...I used often to hear (though not to see) bees. Their murmuring was audible, though their bodily forms were too small to be visible. On inquiry, I found that soot (chiefly from wood and peat) was useful in some stage of their wax or honey manufacture."

IV. The Tortures of Opium

109   "The Tortures of Opium": Baudelaire here combines two chapters of the *Confessions*, "Introduction to the Pains of Opium" and "The Pains of Opium."

110   a very melancholy event: The death of young Catherine Wordsworth.

111   8,000 drops: Or, as De Quincey tells us in the 1856 edition, a quantity that would fill eighty teaspoons.

115   —as when some great painter... eclipse: Shelley, "The Revolt of Islam," V, xxiii, 8–9.

117   Wordsworth's poems: De Quincey identified the poet as Wordsworth only in the 1856 edition.

117   Ricardo's book: David Ricardo (1772–1823), economist and author of *Principles of Political Economy and Taxation* (1817).

118   What a dreadful situation: It is interesting to notice the changes introduced into the text of this passage, in which Baudelaire fuses De Quincey's sentiments with his own. Baudelaire had already discovered the difficulties of composing a work while under the spell of opium. But even as early as 1837, the poet had written of a lethargy that left him feeling dejected and physically exhausted, as he told his brother Alphonse in a letter of 2 November: "My only mistake, or rather mistakes, spring from an eternal indolence, which compels me to postpone each day's labors, so that I am quite unable to set my thoughts to paper, even if only to write to those I care for."

118   the catalog: See p. 135 for Baudelaire's listing of De Quincey's works.

120   Midas changed all things into gold: See "Alchimie de la douleur" in *Les Fleurs du mal*.

120   phenomena: In "Le Poison," in *Les Fleurs du mal*, Baudelaire writes of the powers of expansion incident to opium: "L'opium agrandit ce qui n'a pas de bornes, / Allonge l'illimité, / Approfondit le temps, creuse la volupté, / Et de plaisirs noirs et mornes / Remplit l'âme au delà de sa capacité."

123   the tyranny of the human face: Baudelaire remarked on this phrase in the previous chapter. Cf. "A une heure du matin" (*Le*

Spleen de Paris), in which Baudelaire returns to De Quincey's phrase. Balzac, too, was moved by De Quincey's imagery, to the extent that he used this passage in *La Peau de Chagrin*.

129 "Deeper than ever plummet sounded": *The Tempest*, III, iii, 101.

130 I will sleep no more: *Macbeth*, II, ii, 35.

V. A False Denouement

130 link by link: De Quincey wrote "almost to the final link."

131 "third prostration before the dark idol": From the "Introductory Notice" to the *Suspiria de Profundis*.

132 Jeremy Taylor: De Quincey, having first ascribed this sentiment to Jeremy Taylor, later credited Lord Bacon with this remark, "It is as natural to die as to be born; and to a little infant perhaps the one is as painful as the other."

133 "With dreadful faces throng'd and fiery arms": Milton, *Paradise Lost*, xii, 644.

133 The appendix: To the *Confessions* as published in 1822, De Quincey added an appendix entitled "Unwinding the Accursed Chain." He later rewrote this piece and published it in *Blackwood's* as "Dreaming."

135 a great number of works: This is the "catalog" of works referred to on page 118. De Quincey's work, it should be observed, is eminently that of a magazine contributor. In 'the nineteenth century, most literary works were published first in serial form before they appeared in a bound volume. Baudelaire here lists a representative sample of titles and collections taken from a body of work that fills fourteen volumes. The reader who wishes to become thoroughly familiar with De Quincey's writings should consult the standard edition of his work, *The Collected Writings of Thomas De Quincey* (A. & C. Black, Edinburgh, 1889–90).

136 obituary notice: The *Athenaeum* article of 17 December 1859 reads: "Death has brought a close to the sad and almost profitless career of 'the English Opium-Eater,' removing from the world an intellect that remained active to the last, but had never at any time been of much service to his fellow men, and giving rest to a frame that had paid the penalty of indulgence in prolonged and acute suffering.

"De Quincey has been censured with just severity for want of fidelity to this friends, but the truth is he treated them no worse than he used himself. Endorsing a sentiment of Coleridge's he has remarked in one of his papers, 'Malice is not always of the heart, there is a malice of the understanding and the fancy.' It was his misfortune to exhibit in his writings both forms of malevolence; and he displayed them alike to himself and his old friends indiscriminately and, we believe, at times, unconsciously.

"Coleridge he did not know till 1807, when he made the poet's acquaintance at Bridgewater, in Somersetshire, and contrived to convey to him, through Mr. Cottle's hand, a present of £300. This act of generosity on the part of De Quincey should not be forgotten. *It is true that the time came when, reduced in health and circumstances by his* pernicious *habit of opium-eating, he condescended to accept the charity of others*; and it is also true that he had the indelicacy to allude in his writings to the service he conferred on his friend; *but his conduct on this occasion was noble, though unwise.* The gift was a considerable part of his small patrimony, which had already been much reduced by the expenses of his Oxford life."

136   Pontmartins: Armand de Pontmartin (1811–1890). Pontmartin had reviled Baudelaire's "Edgar Poe, sa vie et ses oeuvres" when it was published as the preface to *Histoires extraordinaires* (March 1856).

136   Beauty is nobler than truth: Baudelaire, in a study of Edgar Allan Poe (*Notes nouvelles sur Edgar Poe*, 1857), quotes the American author's *Hawthorne's "Twice-Told" Tales:* "We have said that the tale has a point of superiority even over the poem. In fact, while the rhythm of this latter is an essential aid in the development of the poem's highest idea—the idea of the Beautiful—the artificialities of this rhythm are an inseparable bar to the development of all points of thought or expression which have their basis in *Truth.*"

36   "Malice is not only of the heart"· The source of these lines is a passage from De Quincey's article "Coleridge and Opium-Eating," published in *Blackwood's Magazine* (1845).

136   a considerable part of his inheritance: De Quincey had made an anonymous gift of £300 to Coleridge.

VI. The Child Genius

136 the *Suspiria:* The *Suspiria de Profundis* (Sighs From the Depths)
first appeared in *Blackwood's Magazine* in March, April, June, and
July 1845. De Quincey published the first four papers, planning
many others, and finally abandoned the work in the middle of
part 2. The *Suspiria* was misleadingly subtitled "Being a Sequel to
the Confessions of an English Opium-Eater."

137 *Mémoires d'outre-tombe:* Chateaubriand's autobiographical masterpiece was written between 1811 and 1841 and published after his
death.

139 relating episodes from his childhood: De Quincey explains: "The
reader must not forget, in reading this and other passages, that,
though a child's feelings are spoken of, it is not the child who
speaks... I the child had the feeling, I the man decipher them."

VII. The Affliction of Childhood

139 "The Affliction of Childhood": First published in *Blackwood's
Magazine* in 1845.

139 horrid pugilistic brothers: In English in Baudelaire's text. De
Quincey writes that his infant feelings "were moulded by the gentlest
of sisters, and not by horrid, pugilistic brothers."

140 *Dulce balneum:* From Baudelaire's own poem, "Franciscæ meæ
laudes" in *Les Fleurs du mal.*

140 *mundi muliebris:* Baudelaire by this comment associates the
reminiscences of his own childhood with those of De Quincey. In a
letter to Poulet-Malassis (23 April 1860), he elaborates: "He loves,
then, his mother, sister, nurse, for the delightful whisper of satin and
fur, for the perfumed throat and hair, for the click of jewelry, for the
rustling ribbons, etc., for all this mundus muliebris...."

143 Memnonian: The stone head of Memnon, in the British Mu-
seum, is reported to have emitted melancholy or cheerful tones as it
was touched by the sun's morning rays.

145 "sublime attractions of the grave": From Wordsworth's *Excursion,*
iv, 238.

145 now applied to animals: In the subsequent portion of De
Quincey's narrative, particulars are given respecting the habits of

sundry animals and household pets, which Baudelaire abridges for the sake of continuity.

VIII. Oxford Visions

147   "Oxford Visions": De Quincey speaks of his Oxford visions in part 2 of the *Suspiria.*

153   Specter of the Brocken: On the nature of that ancient apparition of the Hartz mountains of north Germany, De Quincey writes: "The specter takes the shape of a human figure, or, if the visitors are more than one, then the specters multiply; they arrange themselves on the blue ground of the sky, or the dark ground of any clouds that may be in the right quarter, or perhaps they are strongly relieved against a curtain of rock, at a distance of some miles, and always exhibiting gigantic proportions. At first, from the distance and the colossal size, every spectator supposes the appearance to be quite independent of himself. But very soon he is surprised to observe his own motions and gestures mimicked; and wakens to the conviction that the phantom is but a dilated reflection of himself. . One reason why he is seen so seldom must be ascribed to the concurrence of conditions under which only the phenomenon can be manifested. the sun must be near the horizon;... the spectator must have his back to the sun; and the air must contain some vapour—but *partially* distributed."

153   On... Whitsunday. De Quincey notes, "It is singular, and perhaps owing to the temperature and weather likely to prevail in that early part of summer, that more appearances of the specter have been witnessed on Whitsunday than on any other day."

154   sorcerer's flower: The "sorcerer's flower" and the "sorcerer's altar" are, as De Quincey explains, "names still clinging to the anemone of the Brocken, and to an altar-shaped fragment of granite near one of the summits "

159   I find a note: To "Levana and Our Ladies of Sorrow" as printed in *Blackwood's,* De Quincey added this note: "The reader who wishes at all to understand the course of these Confessions, ought not to pass over this dream-legend. There is no great wonder that a vision, which occupied my waking thoughts in those years, should reappear in my dreams It was in fact a legend recurring in sleep, most of

which I had myself silently written or sculptured in my daylight reveries. But its importance to the present Confessions is this—that it rehearses or prefigures their course. This FIRST part belongs to Madonna. The THIRD belongs to the "Mater Suspiriorum," and will be entitled *The Pariah Worlds.* The FOURTH, which terminates the work, belongs to the "Mater Tenebrarum," and will be entitled *The Kingdom of Darkness.* As to the SECOND, it is an interpolation requisite to the effect of the others; AND will be explained in its proper place." Such was the early outline for the *Suspiria de Profundis.*

Translator's Note

The most difficult problem Baudelaire's "Opium-Eater" poses the translator is its treatment of citations from the sundry writings of De Quincey I have restored these citations where they appear in Baudelaire's work. I have not attempted to alter the archaic diction of the original but have followed De Quincey's texts. Baudelaire at times added his own analysis and altered De Quincey's narrative to better fit his own purpose, thus creating the "amalgam" of which he speaks in his letters He was, for example, under space constraints imposed by his publisher, which led him to cut and summarize the text. Thus, when a series of alterations are too deeply embedded in the text to be disentangled, I have not attempted a deconstruction but have silently incorporated Baudelaire's changes as they occur. If the reader wishes to consult the parallel texts, he will find them in the critical edition of *Un Mangeur d'Opium* (Éditions de la Baconnière, Neuchâtel, 1976). Baudelaire's additions and commentary only are signaled by notes which appear at the back of this volume. It is a remarkable proof of Baudelaire's skill that he made so few translation errors; only a handful are found in "An Opium-Eater." In such cases I have emended, again silently, where the need demands it.

All those who wish to become thoroughly acquainted with the literary production of Thomas De Quincey should consult the only complete edition of this works, that published by Adam and Charles Black (Edinburgh, 1862–1871); this edition was revised by De Quincey.